The Old Lady and the Thief

Coperta: Silvia Ioana Sofineti
Foto: Ciprian Sofineti
Lector: Elena Ciobanu
Redactor: Valeria Manta Tăicuțu
Tehnoredactare: Florin Comăniță

Descrierea CIP a Bibliotecii Naționale a României
SAVIN, VIOREL
   The Old Lady and the Thief / Viorel Savin ; trad.
pieselor în lb. eng. : Mariana Zavati Gardner și Fay
Jacqueline Gardner ; pref. de Elena Ciobanu. –
Râmnicu-Sărat : Valman, 2010
   ISBN 978-606-92272-5-1

   821.135.1-2=111

Tipar: editgraph Buzău
   www.editgraph.ro

Viorel Savin

THE OLD LADY AND THE THIEF

**Translated by: Mariana Zavati Gardner
and Fay Jacqueline Gardner
Introduction: Elena Ciobanu**

VALMAN, 2010

Contents:

Viorel Savin's heroes and their flickering identities

The ultimate test for the value of a play, ever since drama was invented, was that it be acted on stage and find its way into the mind and heart of its audience. As different from poetry or prose, drama depended fundamentally on its relation to its public, therefore, on its pragmatic dimension. The making of meaning in an acted play is not a matter of writing only, but a complex edifice that includes texts, readers, actors and spectators in a mechanism, which is often quite unstable.

Viorel Savin's plays, if one is to judge them by their numerous stage adaptations, in Romania and abroad, have passed the test of success. The author, a prolific playwright and an important figure in the cultural life of Bacău over the last few decades, has also written poetry and prose and has extensively published in many local and national publications. The present volume includes four of his best-known plays (in Mariana Zavati Gardner and Fay Jacqueline Gardner's translation), one of which (*The Old Lady and the Thief*) was first published in 1985, and the other three appeared after 1993. These temporal frames add significant connotations to the plays, taking into account the historical changes that occured in Romania beginning with December 1989.

The texts particularly appeal to a public able to understand the need to escape from an ordinary unbearable existence, which offers only one reason for suffering. Purely existentialist issues are overshadowed by specific significations resulting from the painful memories of a life lived in a type of society that now no longer exists in Romania (and Eastern Europe). Perhaps that is why the dialogues are often soaked in ideology, not only when, for example, they display characters who manifest their hatred against intellectuals (the Petitioner in *The Gate*, the woman's father-in-law in *You Are just a Body*, the Thief in *The Old Lady and the Thief*), but also when some of the characters turn love, art and eternal truth into a sort of hobby-horses for the sake of which they sacrifice everything and everybody (see the Petitioner or Daniil, for instance).

This ideological side in Savin's plays accounts for the fact that his characters do not find themselves in the position to confront complete nothingness and from this point of view they may be considered somehow fortunate. The values they cherish, struggle for or reject form a sort of curtain that separates them from what is truly frightening and that is looming there beyond. Their gestures and deeds are always grounded in this shared system of ideas, and their beliefs are strongly affirmed while they are talking to themselves or to the others. The need to utter one's thoughts, to make them intelligible, to give them a textual form is one of the basic traits of Savin's heroes. Silence is a luxury they can never indulge in for too long, or else they would disappear as subjectivities. Samuel Beckett allows his characters large margins of silence so that both they and the audience feel their despair at the paralyzing emptiness of their existence. Viorel Savin prefers the noise of speech to the terrible wordlessness of his heroes and this sometimes generates a sort of discourse through which the speaker almost too explicitly guides the spectator/reader into the making of a certain meaning.

In *The Gate*, for instance, the Petitioner gives this reply to the Gatekeeper: "You have shown what you are made of: all that courtesy was only lies. Now you are addressing me with 'ye'!" An exchange of remarks follows which is not absolutely necessary for the economy of the text, but whose absence would have created a more troubling depth for both characters. Similarly, in *The Old Lady and the Thief*, the Thief reproaches to the old woman at some point: "Wretched bitch, what are you planning in your head?" This is one version of the same question he repeatedly asks her, thus clearly revealing his loss of control to the audience and encouraging the old lady to go on with

6

her effective stratagem and get rid of him by using his so openly shown vulnerability. Had he manifested his anxiety less obviously, her task would have been less easy and the tension of the scene would have increased considerably.

The author prefers however to dissolve this tension into smaller units, probably in order to emphasize the short, but violent panic attacks experienced by the characters. Another explanation for what one might call Savin's displaced climaxes would be the tenderness that constitutes the best part of these heroes. We are not particularly impressed by their artificial rejection or rebellion against God or by their belief in the superiority of art and truth or by their personal tragedies, but by their gestures of sympathy and warmth. It is not by chance that the author himself makes use of intertextuality in order to enhance the degree of tenderness in his texts. In *Oh Lord, Make Schnauzer Win*, Daniil recites a poem by Sergei Esenin to the new detainee, thereby hoping to show the good intentions and humanity that are hidden underneath his violent words. The heroes' tenderness is only surpassed by their dreaming imagination. In *The Gate*, in a beautiful moment of an intensely poetic value, the Petitioner listens to the mysterious noises of the gate whose mode of existence partakes of a strangeness that suddenly entices the reader: "I wanted to hear how the breeze crosses through it. Through its strings of steel: a giant harp...! Destiny hums through it. It is Everything, I know: it is the Truth! It is the End..."

Daniil's monologues, meant to impress the audience with their solipsistic judgments send, through their semantic ramifications, to such a great Shakespearean hero as Hamlet, whose complex image haunts Daniil's discourse but whose depths are not tapped by Savin's murderer. This happens because the latter's grief is kept into a fatally restricted area of relevance, despite the fact that it touches on the theme of implacable disease and innocent sufferers. Hamlet's spectre only desguises Raskolnikov's (a Raskolnikov without the complicated philosophy of Dostoyevsky's hero), because Daniil's sophisms take him to devious conclusions that blend both sane and perverted ideas, and this makes the reader or the spectator experience pity, rather than terror or identification. The Voice that represents the punishing apparatus is always completely cold and ruthless, and, by association with the guardians methodically beating Daniil, it is made into a symmetrically and unidimensionally constructed opposant to Daniil, whose questions and exclamations thus become the only sign of humanity in the play. Daniil's position is therefore favoured by this created antithesis, his paranoia eventually contaminating the text itself. The final metamorphosis is a sort of 'rhinocerization' (this is Viorel Savin's own way of paying homage to a great precursor, Eugen Ionesco) that leaves one with a feeling of incompleteness and doubt. On the surface, the metaphorical turning of men into cockroaches symbolizes the spiritual corruption of the society, but this is not sufficient for the complete neutralization of Daniil's guilt. His condemnation of the society that punished him for the killing of his wife and daughter (however justified his killing might appear on the surface) is both accepted and rejected by the audience.

The uncertain response Savin's plays trigger in their audience corresponds to the instability of his heroes and heroines. They are artists, actors, workers, convicts or prison guards who are essentially grouped so as they form a complete antagonical couple within which two visions/worlds/categories struggle, communicate or suffocate each other. The protagonists benefit from a very large space of manoeuvre, as compared to the other secondary characters who are often little more than conventionally sketched figures serving the turn of the main characters. Moreover, the type of language heroes and heroines use in Savin's plays functions as a means of individualisation, but not in the same way in which it does in Harold Pinter's plays, for example. Viorel Savin's heroes never forget their grammar – not even when they become rude and aggressive. The violent or even bawdy words they use and invent in order to abuse one another are not only

8

characteristic of the category of rough people, as one might expect. They circulate throughout the entire discourse of all these heroes, functioning as markers of the heroes' incongruences with themselves and of their convoluted emotional developments.

More often than not, guilt is projected onto the other and the truth is almost never faced directly, since the truth would break these heroes' delusions about themselves. Identity is rather avoided, alluded to, and not achieved. The obssession with experiences that should encourage men to step over the threshold into another world is never fully translated into a total transfiguring metamorphosis. The Petitioner does not pass through the gate; the woman in *You Are just a Body*, in spite of the beautiful pantomime she is made to enjoy by the former convict, remains unchanged; the thief and the old lady finally separate in a matter-of-fact chilling dialogue in which she suddenly ignores his existence completely. Daniil, the one who undergoes the negative metaphorical metamorphosis into a cockroach, does not in fact transcend himself – he is only reduced to a number in an absurd universe to which he can never adapt.

The mechanisms that define Viorel Savin's characters are those favouring forgetfulness and concealment, and their physiology plays an important part in this respect. The rebellion against God's will and judgment is coupled with the intense awareness of one's own body: "Man digests, expectorates, urinates, sweats, defecates, salivates, has dandruff, has wax in his ears, has tears in his eyes and, above all, he stinks." says Daniil in *Oh Lord, Make Schnauzer Win*. The impossibility to dissociate one's identity from one's body is, like in the quotation above, sometimes associated with a burst of misanthropy, and sometimes with experiences meant to bring about oblivion or to illustrate one's ideas and justify one's ethically ambiguous deeds. In *The Old Woman and the Thief*, Savin's most successful play by far, the thief describes to the old lady how the very slow chewing of a piece of bread helps him become indifferent and insensitive, how it gives him the opportunity to build a wall around him that separates him from the cruelty he is made to suffer.

Yet the concentration on the life of the body in the hedgehog-killing episode from his childhood reveals something more disturbing. The naturalistic narrative mode of the scene makes it easier for the reader to understand how the suffering brought about by the witnessing of the convulsive body of the incompletely killed animal eventually takes the child who kills it out of pity to an astounding conclusion: "I looked into its eyes, small like beads: people lie; pain can't be read in one's eyes! This will make them feel OK when they torture someone!" This memory is meant to motivate the thief's faltaring behaviour that altarnates gestures of tenderness and brutal reassertions of his status as aggressor in the old lady's house.

The old lady, the best achieved of Savin's characters, is impressive not only because she manages to manipulate the thief, but particularly because she does it so naturally. The thief here is a thief without vocation, his first and most profound need being not to steal and earn money thereby, but to speak about his troubled self to someone who could understand. This is the reason why his insensitive gestures towards the old lady feel so theatrical and forced as compared to his moments of sympathy.

The fluidity and versatility governing the structures of Viorel Savin's plays transforms them into difficult tests for actors, despite the numerous stage directions the author carefully inserts in the text. It is not the physical acting that is at stake, but the actual reconstruction of emotions and thoughts. One can but hope that these plays will always find the actors they deserve.

Elena Ciobanu, PhD
"Vasile Alecsandri" University of Bacău

The Gate - The Initiation
(Poarta - Inițierea)[1]

Characters:

THE GATE
THE GATE KEEPER
THE PETITIONER
THE MESSENGER
JOHANNA - CARLA - THE MOTHER

On the beach, facing the sea, a double metal door, made of wrought iron imitating lances with well-sharpened flat ends, flanked by two simple benches made of wood. A yacht is on the horizon.

The Gate takes part in the conflict due to its own existence, as well as to its screeching, openings - with its own, independent will -, and even to its lifting: Its growth happens in the course of the action.

Noise made by the waves, rustle of grass caused by the song of the grasshoppers.

The Petioner enters.

THE PETITIONER: Good morning.

---

[1] **Printed in the volumes:** „*Doamne, fă ca Schnauzer să câștige!*", Publishing House Casa Scriitorilor, Bacău, 2004; „*Poarta – The Gate*", (bilingual volume, translated into English by Mariana Zavati Gardner), Publishing House Psyhelp, Bacău, 2007.

THE GATEKEEPER *(morose)*: I wish to announce that I'm taking a cut in my wages!

THE PETITIONER: I support that!

THE GATEKEEPER: Why don't you look for somebody else?

THE PETITIONER: My business is over there...! *(He points beyond the Gate)*

THE GATEKEEPER (shouts): Are you mocking at me?

THE PETITIONER: I only said 'Good morning'.

THE GATEKEEPER: Perhaps it might be OK for you, but, as far as I am concerned, I'm nervous... I'm not interested in your opinion.

THE PETITIONER: I didn't say that this nuisance of a day is good for me!

THE GATEKEEPER: But what have you done? I haven't gone yet, I'm still here and I'm not deaf.

THE PETITIONER: Are you dense?

THE GATEKEEPER: You're annoying me!

THE PETITIONER: I've wished you a fine day. In other words, have a fine day!

THE GATEKEEPER: Yes! I hate them! *(surprised)* I happen... to hate, I happen...!

THE PETITIONER: That is... why do you pester me? That is... I only said 'good morning'! What the devil...

THE GATEKEEPER: Do not swear! *(pause)* You're in such a hurry. Look, that's why you have so many problems! You cannot say that a day is good or, if it were to be good, you can say this only after it ended.

THE PETITIONER: I respect the custom.

THE GATEKEEPER: The custom is wrong! Do not bother me any more! As the day is unfolding, do not come here to tell me that the day is good, that it is extraordinary, that it is sticky with pink cream. That makes me feel like I'm flying into a rage. Moreover, I'm not responsible for my actions! Do you get my drift?

THE PETITIONER:....?

THE GATEKEEPER: At least, if you care about yourself, you may ask me, 'Is it good?' - The Day, I mean! Just in case, you have any common sense.

THE PETITIONER: I just intend to ask you this. Of course, after I have greeted you first. Therefore...!

THE GATEKEEPER: No!

THE PETITIONER: What, 'no'?

THE GATEKEEPER: 'No' is the answer to the stupid question which you rubbed through the grease of your sleepy brain.

THE PETITIONER. Well, as if I haven't asked you any questions!

THE GATEKEEPER: Recognize, do you think I am a cretin?

THE PETITIONER: God forbid! However, I dare not even think of such a thing! I do not insult people! Especially when it is obvious that I need them.

THE GATEKEEPER: In this case, which... I hardly bear...!

THE PETITIONER: I am warning you: you must be very, very prudent with me!

THE GATEKEEPER: ...In case, which I can merely bear!... listen... imagine even... that I cannot guess why you, a naïve idler, are here in front of me?

THE PETITIONER: For... *(He points beyond the gate)*

THE GATEKEEPER: Have I told you? I knew! It hasn't been seen...?

THE PETITIONER: So what, if you knew?

THE GATEKEEPER: You aren't very clever...

THE PETITIONER: Hey, see where you go: whom are you talking to?... Stinking peasant!

THE GATEKEEPER: I wanted to explain why I replied "no": I was brief. Nevertheless, you prefer empty words, and lots of them! Do you really believe that you could

13

hide behind so many words? That they could nurse hypocrisy… If you had any respect for the Word, you could easily learn that… lots of Words represent a greater un-known territory!

THE PETITIONER: I summon you for the last time: behave in a civilized manner!

THE GATEKEEPER: I apologize for doubting your intelligence, but it is not entirely my fault.

THE PETITIONER: I denounce you!

THE GATEKEEPER: Whom to?

THE PETITIONER: Step aside!

THE GATEKEEPER: Calm down.

THE PETITIONER: Aside from my path, castrated cockerel!

THE GATEKEEPER: Calm down.

THE PETITIONER: Aside, macaque!

THE GATEKEEPER: Oi!

THE PETITIONER: What did you say? *(He chokes in disgust)*

THE GATEKEEPER: I said "oi".

THE PETITIONER: How dare you, blockhead!

THE GATEKEEPER: So that I make you understand.

THE PETITIONER: You?!... A non-entity! You stinking gatekeeper! You intellectual filth. Kaghebache! You routine trap. You stick-in-the-mud! It is…!

(The Gatekeeper throws a fist full of sand into his eyes. The Petitioner, blinded)

THE PETITIONER: What are doing, you idiot?

THE GATEKEEPER: Stop it! You are boring.

(The blinded Petitioner stoops down, wipes his eyes, he cries. The Gatekeeper sits on the bench, on the right. Only The Petioner's sobs can be heard. Then, silence.

The Gatekeeper is chewing a piece of grass while he is checking the performance hall with a searchlight connected to the electricity socket of the Gatepost. He stares at a spectator, he focuses, he becomes anxious, then he gives up, etc.
For a while, The Petitioner follows him, in anticipation. Then, believing he could win, he runs to the gates, he tries to open them, he hits them with his fists, with his feet, he screams)

THE PETITIONER: Let me go!... Take me outside!... Receive me! Open, I want you!... I am alone!

(The Gatekeeper follows him calmly; he knocks him to the ground with a kick. He begins to kick him methodically, rolling him without pity, up to the front of the stage, at the same time, scrutinising the bodies and the faces of the people in the audience with the searchlight. While The Gatekeeper is calmly performing this activity - he is displaying a certain boredom in his gestures and a precision that shows routine - Johanna turns up in an electric wheelchair)

THE PETITIONER: Johanna?! You, here? Why?
JOHANNA: You were always fascinated by extreme situations. Be happy! (…) Is he hitting you terribly? Why don't you tell him that you love him for that? After all, all your life, and without exception, you loved all those who wronged you. - And it wasn't even out of Christian love: it was out of cowardly love.
THE PETITIONER *(from the ground)*: It's not true! My revolt has always been frozen by their honest reasons!...
JOHANNA: How many tears of despair I poured out, seeing how you worshipped your executioners! Their will

dissolved you; you even acted against your principles...
Then you suffered.

THE PETITIONER: I hated them! But I could not hit them, because they believed in their own honesty! Is this my fault that they knew they were honest and that they were acting honestly, according to their own consciousness?!...

JOHANNA: How fair and honest has Ioana been?

THE PETITIONER: I had a marriage contract with her. I was tied up.

JOHANNA: Tied up by a barren shrew? You hypocrite!...

THE PETITIONER: I have always respected the law.

JOHANNA: Formally. With me, you have conceived Carla, during the weekends and you did not seem to be shaken by any prejudice. On the contrary, the lovemaking you showed me...

THE PETITIONER: You interpreted it wrongly: you were the most...

JOHANNA: My dear, I was! I always was, rarely have I had the joy of being!...

THE PETITIONER: You were my only love.

JOHANNA: That is why you were enthusiastically paying my rent, but going out, to shows, to exhibitions, you were with your wife. An unfortunate nymphomaniac with dry ovaries. - Look, I contaminated myself with your language... I loved you enormously.

THE PETITIONER: and I!

JOHANNA: You don't even realise you are lying. I know you so well... However, I don't regret...!

THE PETITIONER: I cried a lot.

JOHANNA: When? When I slipped on the rocks of the cliff, or later, when I had a heart attack?

THE PETITIONER: I cried for all our sorrows, Johanna. For your fall from the cliffs and for your heart attack and for Carla's awful situation and our extended separations...

JOHANNA: You have been near whores for too long...! *(The Gatekeeper continues to hit him.)* What an excessive blow he gave you! It is now the moment for you tell him you love him. Go on, tell him, and respect your wise program of existence... A dignified and unique existance, my beloved dear and stupid man...!

THE PETITIONER: After you left...

JOHANNA: After I had the happiness of dying!

THE PETITIONER: I took Carla to my house.

JOHANNA: You took her to meet your parents! Secretively! You gave her your name, you brave man, only after that slut - I learnt it from you, do not scold me! -, had abandoned you and ran to Marseille with that hysteric little actor; there you sent them money like an idiot, a right cretin, - I borrowed the right words from you too -, to enable them to get out of the French jail! That's who you are! And now, kiss the ass of that gentleman who is sorting you out so beautifully! But you... You love your executioners! *(She leaves)*

THE PETITIONER *(calls in despair)*: JOHANNAaaa! I loved you!

JOHANNA: Anyway, this does not comply with your existential programme: I was always kind to you. At least...you can hate me. *(She disappears)*

(The Gatekeeper finishes his "job", he collects his electric cable, and he sits on the bench once again)

THE PETITIONER *(admiringly, sorting out his clothes)*: You hit well. You are good. Good, good!

THE GATEKEEPER *(modestly)*: I try my best. It's my trade!

THE PETITIONER: I see...!

THE GATEKEEPER: But of course.

THE PETITIONER: You made me turn blue all over! You succeeded: now, I have become another, I belong to the Blue Race!... Are you enjoying yourself?

THE GATEKEEPER: I do my duty with a sense of responsibility, with pride and with high professionalism!

THE PETITIONER: Don't you take any pity?

THE GATEKEEPER: An order is an order!

THE PETITIONER: Don't you take pity at all? At all, at all?...

THE GATEKEEPER: Dear Sir, to me, pity, is only... a unit of measurement.

THE PETITIONER: I guess that is the one with the subdivisions: understanding, generosity and gentleness.

THE GATEKEEPER: You are wrong, Sir: I am referring to the other pity! The one with the subdivisions of metre, centimetre, and millimetre. I remain immune by being practical. So that... *(Menacingly)* you see!...

THE PETITIONER: Therefore, you haven't.

THE GATEKEEPER: What, Mister, haven't I got?

THE PETITIONER: Pity.

THE GATEKEEPER: Well - this together with endurance and charity, I told you I haven't got them. No... I have!

THE PETITIONER *(hoping, gesture toward the Gate)*: When I arrive...

THE GATEKEEPER: Not a 'when I arrive'! When you succeed in thinking like me, you'll have the right to replace me.

THE PETITIONER: This, never!

THE GATEKEEPER: Ho, ho, ho, ho...! You have uttered a lie...! The first!

THE PETITIONER *(recites):*
'Unaccompanied and alone -
Uniquely withdrawn
Isolated

18

Exclusive wilderness
Solitary!

Stray
Only I
Hidden wanderer -
Absurd nothingness
Alienated and alone...'

THE GATEKEEPER: Ha, ha, ho, ho!... You have composed, how naive you are! A tautological poem!... You are a sorry player!

THE PETITIONER: I recited from 'The Fall'. An equally sad play like the one we are performing now... And... I am put out more by a hero's image than by that of a spectator's. To be a hero is risky... And with a predictable end.

(The Gatekeeper stands up suddenly, picks up part of a branch, which he plants into the soil)

THE PETITIONER: You pretend that I don't matter to you, but I feel that I do. You have your agenda, which you are hiding from me, proof of the apparent polite manner in which you talk to me. If you know your interest, you are intruding into my space! You have nothing to lose, on the contrary: in case of an emergency, you will have a grateful friend...

THE GATEKEEPER: Stop this rubbish!... And now, a warning: do not approach the Gate farther than this sign! Is this clear to you? You must not go any farther than this, on no account.

THE PETITIONER: But I wish, at least, to see the Gate from close up! I have wanted this for such a long time...!

THE GATEKEEPER: You can see it very well from over there.

THE PETITIONER: I am shortsighted.

THE GATEKEEPER: Like hell you are! The Lord forgives me for you have contaminated me…! But how have you reached the idea that you must force it?

THE PETITIONER: I wanted… to hear it.

THE GATEKEEPER: …?

THE PETITIONER: I wanted to hear how the breeze crosses through it. Through its strings of steel: a giant harp…! Destiny hums through It. It is Everything, I know: it is the Truth! It is the End…

THE GATEKEEPER: If you dare to go past this pole even with your ears, I shall cut them! Without that pity that you like so much and which was invented by blockheads.

THE PETITIONER: I am grateful even for this. For the time being, this is enough for me.

(He drags himself on his belly, he places his ear close to the branch-sign stuck in the sand, he stays like that for a while, then, he suddenly turns, his feet to the Gate, in an attempt to touch it)

THE GATEKEEPER *(he stands up enraged)*: Listen, what have we decided together?

THE PETITIONER: But I did not take my ear off the sign you have put. Don't be unjust, respect your own rules!

THE GATEKEEPER: Are you an utter fool?

THE PETITIONER: I am intelligent. *(He laughs satisfied)*: He, he, he!...

THE GATEKEEPER: You laugh like an ass.

THE PETITIONER: How does an ass laugh?

THE GATEKEEPER: Well, what was I saying? You are laughing just like that. Ha, ha, ha…!

THE PETITIONER: Ho, ho, ho! You are good, you harsh creature. You are qualified! What a figure you cut, Mr. Gatekeeper, what's your name?I…

(Creaking)

THE GATEKEEPER: Shush!

(The two parts of the Gate set jar)

THE PETITIONER: Is someone coming?
THE GATEKEEPER (whisper): Be quiet.

(The two parts of the Gate close back, and then they set ajar once again)

THE PETITIONER: Scented effluvia are coming from that direction, surely they must accompany someone important!...
THE GATEKEEPER: I told you to be quiet!
THE PETITIONER *(he points beyond the Gate)*: Is there the paradise?
THE GATEKEEPER: Be quiet please!...
THE PETITIONER: There is our good, there is all we have dreamt, and there is the future...! There...
THE GATEKEEPER: Bother, will you be quiet, after all, gasbag that you are!
THE PETITIONER *(startled, surprised)*: I don't allow that!
THE GATEKEEPER: Do not allow your godMOTHER, you fool, who attended to your farting! *(The gatekeeper pulls him by the ear to the front of the stage; the patitioner hits his head onto the ground.)* Learn! Learn! Learn! Learn: for three times, learn! *(Carla walks in: a very beautiful girl dressed in the latest teenage fashion)*
CARLA: You haven't learnt anything from me, your daughter, and I wasn't stupid at all... Father, you acted very mean!...

THE PETITIONER: I was desperate, CARLA.

CARLA: To ask the police to follow me? What, have I stolen something, have I committed murder? Have I prostituted myself?

THE PETITIONER: Watch what you say! After I finish here, I'll follow you and I'll smack you soundly!

CARLA: That's all you know. 'I'll smack you' – 'Go back to your seat' – 'You are not allowed!' - "You are not allowed **to do**, you are not allowed **to go to,** you are not allowed **to see**! The jail is in the middle of my family, in the centre of the town where I was born! I cannot find anything else, only interdictions in this house!

THE PETITIONER: You ran away from home, and I am responsible. I am res-pon-si-ble for your future, intelligence of the world!

CARLA: Then, if this future, which you ram down my throat, is mine, let it belong to me! Don't supervise it! Don't plan it, don't modify it according to your way of being and understanding: I am an adult now, don't you understand? I have periods and I can make babies...

THE PETITIONER: Carla!!...

CARLA: ...as many as I wish for! How I wish for and where I wish for, if you meddle into my life!

THE PETITIONER: I have asked for the assistance of the police out of despair.

CARLA (*she screams*): Those beasts had interrogated and beaten up all my friends. All of them, and the innocent ones, who were tortured for hours on end, were menaced and were locked up because of me!... Why am I the only one you got out of jail? But I also smoked grass in their company! How can I ever look them in the eye? I have not injected cocaine, but as soon as my friends get out...

THE PETITIONER: Yours?!...

CARLA: Yes, mine! As soon as they get out of the trouble you landed them in, and they get out!, because they did not kill anybody, I shall do my first injection! So you know. And then, we leave!

THE PETITIONER: Where are you going, daddy's girl?

CARLA: I am not telling you, because you will grass on us.

THE PETITIONER: Do you hate me?

CARLA *(calm)*: Because of you, we cannot communicate normally.

THE PETITIONER: I wish nothing else for you, but a secure career! That's why I'll do everything within my power, even if I do it wrong.

CARLA: Fuck you!

THE PETITIONER: You insolent girl!

CARLA: So what, do you think it hurts? I have become practical. We don't deceive one another with the achievements of your sick society: we return to nature!

THE PETITIONER: With those scruffy wasters, washed by summer rains only?!

CARLA: The happiness to be one with Nature, to return to where you left... a long time ago, without being questioned if you wish to be amongst people...! Could there be greater happiness than mending the terrible mistake of having become a human being?...

THE PETITIONER: If you grant me a little more time, Carla... Don't decide on your own. You belong to me! I love you...

CARLA: I have seen how your love goes, when you say you love: what did you do to MOTHER?

THE PETITIONER: I loved your MOTHER enormously.

CARLA: In bed, yes. *(She taps her chest with her fingers)* Look what a great result has come out of your love: a fruit infested with grubs, which you will bury in the Amazon jungle, as soon as possible! *(She is crying)* The fruit that I am... Oh Lord, it will sprout from the soil and it will also bear fruit, but in a manner, I hope Lord, more fitting than until now.

THE PETITIONER: No, Carla, don't decide until you know…! *(He cries)*

CARLA: Nevertheless I love you. Now, I leave you. For good.

THE PETITIONER: You have promised to wait… for your friends, in order to…!

CARLA: Yes, I shall wait for them to make the journey together, but I shall not wait for them here: I must defend myself. I am an adult, but you are a late developing adolescent, you have not got the strength to notice this. I guess that… your dreams divide us! I am sorry, but you trully deserve this. *(She disappears)*

THE PETITIONER: I don't allow you…! *(To The Gatekeeper)* I don't allow you!

THE GATEKEEPER: Nobody tells me what is allowed and what is not allowed. Because I know1 Listen well! I am struggling with you, I sweat, I make an effort, but in vain…! *(He turns; with his foot, he knocks over the branch stuck into the sand)* I am ready to swear!…

THE PETITIONER: Why are you getting rid of the sign? We have agreed! You are not keeping your word. You are a crook! You villain!

THE GATEKEEPER: I have allowed you too much: you are unable to stop where you should and when you should…

THE PETITIONER *(mean)*: Do you want chocolate?

THE GATEKEEPER: Are you trying to bribe me?

THE PETITIONER: I am asking you again: do you want it?

THE GATEKEEPER: I have diabetes. This… is it called 'a bribe'?

THE PETITIONER: Everybody takes it. Why wouldn't you also take it?

THE GATEKEEPER: You won't understand.

THE PETITIONER: But some... exotic fruit? Fresh, what do you say about that? Just arrived: mango?

THE GATEKEEPER: I have an ulcer.

THE PETITIONER: An ulcer?!... Then, genuine Russian vodka, vintage, from about the middle of the last century: it is all that is needed for a cauterization... like at her MOTHER's!

THE GATEKEEPER: For God's sake, don't you understand that I am like a Schweitzer? I have holes in my duodenum! I am like a sieve.

THE PETITIONER: But... some green banknotes? Well?... A handsome sum...! You can do whatever you want with them.

THE GATEKEEPER: Perfectly agreed! Are you pleased?

THE PETITIONER: No.

THE GATEKEEPER: Mr. 'No' has died because of how stupid he was, because he was too greedy!

THE PETITIONER: You are as thick as two short planks. With education!...

THE GATEKEEPER: You've got a lot to learn: one is happy only when one is happy with what one has got!

THE PETITIONER: Rubbish. You have been uttering only garbage since I met you!

THE GATEKEEPER: Correct! Look, you are the perfect example of unhappiness: you want a lot, much more, even more...! And then you complain of solitude.

THE PETITIONER: Do you know that the dam high above the town has collapsed? No, you have not realised because the river flows behind the hill. The flood has razed everything: ruins! The children were taken by the waves; the elders alike, only those who could fight with the waters escaped with their lives. The purpose of their lives, their children... vanished. All was lost. Everything went down the drain; don't you feel anything?

THE GATEKEEPER: What do you want me to feel? I feel joy! If those able are alive, they will make other children: people are as busy as a bee when they enjoy their work.

THE PETITIONER *(He shouts):* But their children died!?...

THE GATEKEEPER: One doesn't know what they might have become. Surely that many future criminals also drowned...

THE PETITIONER: You are cynical.

THE GATEKEEPER: The situation exists... could be qualified as wonderful.

THE PETITIONER *(he is demonstrating, he is calling slogans):* Down with stu-pi-di-ty... Down with stu-pi-di-ty... Down with stu-pi-di-ty... Huooo!...

THE GATEKEEPER: You should also see the good side of things.

THE PETITIONER: Huo, you liar!...

THE GATEKEEPER: People, now, have a more complex purpose, to rebuild...

THE PETITIONER: Down with state terrorism! Down with villains!

THE GATEKEEPER: To breed, to ensure their children's survival...!

THE PETITIONER: To jail with fascists!... Huo!... Down with the nationalists from the left! Down with the nationalists from the centre! Down with the nationalists from the right! Long live the liberty of conscience!...

THE GATEKEEPER: They had everything until yesterday: they were stuffing themselves, they were plagued by the vice of indolence, and they had no expectations.

THE PETITIONER: Down with stupi-dity, down with stupi-dity, down with stupi-dity!...

THE GATEKEEPER: Ho!

THE PETITIONER: Again?...

THE GATEKEEPER: Why haven't you turned up here until now, to cross *(Gesture in the direction of the Gate)* onto the other side?

THE PETITIONER *(surprised):* Because something so grievous, like what I have just told you now, has never happened before!

THE GATEKEEPER: You see? You agree with me now: you have a purpose.

THE PETITIONER: Sophisms in bad taste...

THE GATEKEEPER: Yes, yes: now you live to the full! You feel you pulsate with life. What did you do until yesterday?

THE PETITIONER: I am an artist.

THE GATEKEEPER: And this very moment, well, well, well, well... In what capacity are you here?

THE PETITIONER: Here...I don't know who I am. I don't know any longer...!

THE GATEKEEPER: Very productive: look, you are forced to search. **To search for yourself!** There are signs telling that you are beginning to understand that you have succeeded in becoming another and... look: you do not know yourself. You have a purpose at last! A programme! Who is like you? You feel important, you have become somebody, but... you need recognition. **Recognition!** This exists only *(He points to the Gate)* there! Ha, haaa!... And however... Your altruism is only an ordinary selfishness. *(Suddenly, harsh)* Back! Back, do not try one of your manoeuvres again; otherwise, I shall squash you! I shall obliterate you! Nothing sickens me more than a change of labels. Be sure do not try this again: the Gate is sacred! Learn this too!

THE PETITIONER: I am sorry...!

THE GATEKEEPER: How will you benefit if I forgave you?

THE PETITIONER: I shall be more relaxed. Can you forgive me? No?... Try! Make an effort for a poor fellow. That is for me.

THE GATEKEEPER: Still selfish!...

THE PETITIONER: But, altruistic: so that I can act efficiently, not for any other reason, don't you understand? For the benefit of both of us: I escape, you... get rid of me...!

THE GATEKEEPER: Altruistic, my foot...! Mr. and all of you lot, where have come from? The world is full of people like you! What do you feed on so that there are so many of you, and so resistant? Damn you!...

THE PETITIONER: Well, I realise I must give up. *(He leaves)*

THE GATEKEEPER: Wait!

THE PETITIONER *(He stops):* I said I was leaving, and I am leaving! The rubbish you've delivered convinced me and... I had enough of it. 'To wish for more is a proof of poverty. The wise person desires only what he / she needs, and, when he / she gets what he / she wants... he / she is happy!...'

THE GATEKEEPER: No: 'to be happy, you need to be content with what you have!'

THE PETITIONER: Intellectual rubbish. I am dying of pleasure, am I not!

THE GATEKEEPER: ...Before you return to where you came from, try to guess what this means:

> 'To any house,
> I am a chosen servant;
> I welcome anyone
> Who happens to visit;
> When they leave
> I accompany them again' -
> What am I?

THE PETITIONER: I don't know.

28

THE GATEKEEPER: And... you wish to go through what you don't know?!... Could you be so imprudent?... It is the Gate!

THE PETITIONER: Repeat the test!

THE GATEKEEPER: 'To any house, / I am a chosen servant; / I welcome anyone / Who happens to visit; / When they leave / I accompany them again" –
What am I?'

THE PETITIONER: So: a servant to the house... welcomes... when someone arrives and when someone leaves... The answer is: the door!

THE GATEKEEPER: You are so absent-minded...! I have just told you: it is the gate!

THE PETITIONER: But it is the DOOR! You don't understand even what you know by heart already.

THE GATEKEEPER: You must understand the difference: the house is big, that's why it has also got several doors, and there is the question of 'a servant' and not of 'servants'. And then, it is clearly stated: 'To any house, / I am a chosen servant' – 'house', with its comprehensive meaning of property: with a master, with outbuildings, everything! Plus, the authority. Therefore, it is clear: we are talking... of... the gate.

THE PETITIONER: Damn it!... All that is uncomplicated... is brilliant.

THE GATEKEEPER: Therefore, recognize that you wished to go through something you did not know!

THE PETITIONER: I guess so. But I have an excuse: I don't know enough.

THE GATEKEEPER: Do you believe, as it were, do you doubt or did you certainly wish to commit a blameable act?

THE PETITIONER *(he screams)*: Yessss!

THE GATEKEEPER *(sighs with relief)*: It isss... always the first step...! It was difficult to make it.

THE PETITIONER: Towards what?

THE GATEKEEPER: Towards accomplishment!

THE PETITIONER: May I go through it now?

THE GATEKEEPER: Where to?

THE PETITIONER: To the other side.

THE GATEKEEPER: No.

(Silence. One could grasp a sizzling)

THE PETITIONER: I can hear something.

THE GATEKEEPER: Yes.

THE PETITIONER: Are there snakes?

THE GATEKEEPER: The Time.

THE PETITIONER: ...?

THE GATEKEEPER: A hungry time: is eating away at the Gate. The rust... The rust is eating it away.

THE PETITIONER: Is this what is fizzy?

THE GATEKEEPER *(angry):* It is you who is fizzy. The Gate is... sizzling! It is fighting. The Time is covering it in verdigris, it is oxidizing it, and it is burning it! The Gate is afraid!...

THE PETITIONER: What could a gate be frightened of?

THE GATEKEEPER: Would ye be happy to end up as a... wreck? A rusty wreck, without flesh, without muscles, without... Ye are fizzy with joy, aren't ye? Because ye are melting with every second!... Or because ye are fretting like a hare in a trap? Have ye heard how a trapped in a snare hare sounds like? All its life, it has never made a sound until then?!

THE PETITIONER: Until the end, you have not resisted. You have shown what you are made of: all that courtesy was only lies. Now you are addressing me with "ye"!

THE GATEKEEPER: Is this disturbing ye?

THE PETITIONER: This is nothing compared to the beating, which you administered me earlier and which nearly killed me.

THE GATEKEEPER: This nothing has done ye a lot of good: This means that I begin to appreciate ye... When I despise someone, I use the pronoun of politeness 'you' in order to keep the scoundrels at a great distance. - I hate to have words put into my mouth.

THE PETITIONER: Therefore I am no scoundrel.

THE GATEKEEPER: On the contrary, ye might be! The advantage is that I am not so sure now.

THE PETITIONER: Has someone told you that you are stuffed with money?

THE GATEKEEPER: Ha, ha, ha, ha!...

(Spreading noise of a cane pulled from the mud, and of cracking bones)

THE PETITIONER *(He throws himself on his belly)*: The Earth is moving. Earthquake! It had started in the same wat as when the dam collapsed... In the same way!...

THE GATEKEEPER: Look and nothing will happen to ye... Nothing.

THE PETITIONER: The Sea will collapse over us! Look, the yacht is bobbing up and down! Look how the waves shake it.

THE GATEKEEPER: Sit down and look at it.

THE PETITIONER *(He screams):* What should I look at?

THE PETITIONER: The Gate is growing. If ye are quiet and understand, ye become wise.

(Indeed, the Gate is projected by means of telescopic devices – it 'is growing' vertically)

THE PETITIONER: Fantastic!...

THE GATEKEEPER: Ye thought ye knew it all.

THE PETITIONER: It's not true…!

THE GATEKEEPER: Of course ye don't know. That's it, quiet, now.

(they look in silence at how the Gate is rising on the background of the Sea: it is evening, it is morning, and it is day again. The majestic Gate overwhelms the space)

THE PETITIONER: Once again: Please forgive me.

THE GATEKEEPER: Do ye feel a better person now?

THE PETITIONER: Much better.

THE GATEKEEPER: I forgive ye.

THE PETITIONER: I shall never forget this!

THE GATEKEEPER: Do ye also forgive me?

THE PETITIONER: Yes.

THE GATEKEEPER: Good. Ye have already stepped over a threshold.

THE PETITIONER: Due to ye.

THE GATEKEEPER: Due to those who have taught me.

THE PETITIONER: Ye are their representative.

THE GATEKEEPER: Their servant only.

THE PETITIONER: Are we going to cross?

THE GATEKEEPER: Where to?

THE PETITIONER: To the Gate.

THE GATEKEEPER: It is time.

(A pagan ritual is performed)

THE PETITIONER: Shall I recite Guillaume de Saint-Thierry's text?

THE GATEKEEPER: It is the most suitable (He is kneeling).

THE PETITIONER *(He gets nearer the Gate, he touches It, he kisses his fingers, he touches the Earth, and he lifts*

32

his arms towards the horizon): Oh, you who said: I am the Gate…

THE GATEKEEPER: The Gate…

THE PETITIONER: …Gate, show us clearly to what dwelling you belong.

THE GATEKEEPER: Gate.

THE PETITIONER: …Gate. When and for whom will you open? What house are you a gate to?

THE GATEKEEPER: You are the Gate to the House of the Heavens…

THE GATEKEEPER: And of the Sea.

THE PETITIONER: It is the Sea where your Father lives. Why the Sea?

THE GATEKEEPER: I guess that it is better how ye said the first time.

THE PETITIONER: The house to which the Gate belongs to is in the sky where your Father is. Amen!

THE GATEKEEPER: Amen. *(He stands up).* Listen now to what Evseev is saying: *(He is singing)* The gates attached to the fence at the entrance to the yard represent, from a genetic point of view, a contamination of the scheme of ancestral tombs on supports!... The Gate is 'a cart', the Gate is 'the dowry box', and the Gate is 'the coffin'! *(To The Petitioner)* What else could the dove above the gates be than the symbol of the extraterrestrial tomb from which dove-souls fly?

THE PETITIONER: Ameeen!...

THE GATEKEEPER: No, go on!...

THE PETITIONER: I go on: Ameeen!...

(The Gatekeeper moves his hand with a gesture showing he is fed up, he gathers a bunch of aromatic plants, sets fire to them, he makes signs with a chalk on the supports of the Gate, he smokes It according to a ritual, while

33

performing an unusual dance with a complicated choreography.
The Petitioner decorates It with crowns made of plants, he places burdock and liana in flower, sloe and rose berries in front of It.)

THE PETITIONER: Thorns keep away ghosts!

(They hold hands, staring at the horizon)

THE GATEKEEPER: If you stare at the yacht, if you try not to blink, you'll notice it is moving.
THE PETITIONER: I see it move from where I stand.
THE GATEKEEPER: You are well received!
THE PETITIONER: I feel very weak. Of happiness and gratitude?
THE GATEKEEPER: Let's see if you might bring THE MESSENGER. Then... we'll talk later.
THE PETITIONER: What Messenger?
THE GATEKEEPER *(to himself):* I hope that you'll be able to see him.

(He moves the benches away; he stacks them on top of one another on the left side of the stage)

THE PETITIONER: Have you tried to gaze farther than the yacht?
THE GATEKEEPER: I am trying in my soul.
THE PETITIONER: ...? ...What are you making?
THE GATEKEEPER: An altar. We shall pray that It *(He points to the Gate)* will put in a good word. For us... We are in great need, do you know...
THE PETITIONER: In this case, you should place the bench from the left to the base of the altar...
THE GATEKEEPER: Ntztztz! *(He is working)*

THE PETITIONER: Because you are becoming stubborn, aren't you! I also want to contribute.

THE GATEKEEPER: The benches are not placed as someone fancies! The bench from the right is always placed underneath.

THE PETITIONER: Where is it written that the altar of the Gate should be made by placing the bench from the right underneath and above the one from the left?

THE PETITIONER: Could you not bother me? I do as I know best and let's leave it to this!

THE PETITIONER: But at least do as I say for once! *(He hurries, he knocks over the benches, he places above the bench that was underneath, etc.)* Damn it!

THE GATEKEEPER: I told you not to swear!

THE PETITIONER: Damn you!

(The Gatekeeper hits him in the face with his fist so hard that he rolls to the ground)

THE GATEKEEPER: I told you for the last time!

(Quietly, the Petitioner touches his face full of blood)

THE GATEKEEPER: I do not like to repeat myself! I have warned you.

(He rebuilds the improvised construction. Behind him, the Petitioner runs, he grabs the bench and hits him hard on the head. The Gatekeeper faints.
The Petitioner looks at him for a moment, he gathers his things, he steals The Gatekeeper's lantern, and he runs to the Gate, he tries to open it, but he does not succeed. He leans upon it with his chest and raised arms. He stares in the distance. The yacht returns to the point of departure)

THE PETITIONER: Oh Lord, let me pass! My torn patience gives birth to questions and I do not know what I should do. If I could pass, I shall redeem. *(He shouts)* Open yourself to me and I shall praise you when I enter... Help me...! It is said that the Gate withdraws into the earth when those who are good indulge in love, and in all that is earthly and rises when someone yearns to reach there... I grew when I arrived... *(He looks at the knocked over Gatekeeper)*. I say, rise! What have I done, my Lord?!...

(He places the items back from where he took them - in order to hide his attempt of running away - he kneels near the Gate)

THE PETITIONER: I have not killed him, have I?

(He turns the Gatekeeper face up, he presses his chest rhythmically, trying to resuscitate him, he decides: He gives him mouth-to-mouth resuscitation. The Gatekeeper recovers, he grabs the Petitioner from behind his shoulders, he rolls him and he climbs onto him kissing him on his face, on his neck...)

THE PETITIONER: Let me be. Let me be. Are you mad? I say, you cretin!!...

THE GATEKEEPER *(panting):* It is a long time since I met a woman!

THE PETITIONER: But I am not a skirt, lusty bull!

THE GATEKEEPER: You kissed me in my sleep!

THE PETITIONER: To... to... To wake you up!

THE GATEKEEPER: I am flattered. But if you are not going... further, don't do it again. I am a man... you should understand...!

36

THE PETITIONER: I was wrong, OK?

THE GATEKEEPER: But, you love me. A little, a little... After all, I am shoulder to shoulder with you, am I not?

THE PETITIONER: You are... you are... likable!

THE GATEKEEPER: And you are too!... I shall give you a nice present. I remember, I don't forget: I am an attentive person with... friends...

THE PETITIONER: Please forget about it!

THE GATEKEEPER: I remember everything! This is my job. *(He holds him by his shoulders)*. Let's build the altar... Both of us! Which bench do we have to place at the base?

THE PETITIONER: The one that was on the right of the Gate.

THE GATEKEEPER *(looking at him languishingly)*: No... the one that was placed on the left... I would like you to be content.

THE PETITIONER: Good, let's finish: the one that was placed on the left!

THE GATEKEEPER: OK. *(He gazes at him)*. You have a kind face, with soft skin, as if it were a fresh fruit...!

THE PETITIONER: What shall we do, after we finish arranging the benches?

THE GATEKEEPER: Do you wish to suggest something?

THE PETITIONER *(revolted)*: We must finish the altar!

THE GATEKEEPER: A...! Yes, of course, I am going to look for some ornamental plants. And you?

THE PETITIONER: I can draw! I would like to make an icon with the image of the Gate set ajar.

THE GATEKEEPER: Excellent idea! Look in the bag: there are some coloured crayons and some cardboard in that box near the lantern. When I was alone, I pencilled in various notes to myself... Use them...

THE PETITIONER: These ones?

THE GATEKEEPER: Yes. What beautiful hands you have!... Do not be ashamed. They are yours...! I wish you to make headway. I shall bring you some wormwood and some wild thyme. Don't worry: They are for fumigation and for perfume. Bye! Bye...

THE PETITIONER *(to himself)*: Paranoiac! *(Aloud)*: Aren't you afraid to leave me alone? *(He points to the Gate)*

THE GATEKEEPER *(smiling affectionately)*: Now, I know for certain that you won't leave. You have proven to me that you don't want to leave any longer. (He exits)

(The Petitioner gazes after him, he starts to draw. He is absorbed by his work. A strange vivid music, of forge and hammer, of bones and skulls can be heard, accompanied by the roar of an earthquake: The Gate is growing. The Petitioner looks at it serenely, smiling happily. He is working)

THE PETITIONER: Will you open, a little, for me? No? When you wish, You will do it! I understand and...I am quiet. I am so glad I have not given it up...! When you wish: I am not in a hurry.

(On the horizon, the yacht is moving again to the right. The Petitioner finishes his drawing; he places it on the stacked benches. The Gatekeeper enters with plants and herbs in flower)

THE GATEKEEPER: Are you ready?
THE PETITIONER: Here it is!
THE GATEKEEPER: Is this an icon? Are you mocking at me? It looks like a mitre.
THE PETITIONER: This is how you see it!
THE GATEKEEPER: This is how it is.

THE PETITIONER: A mitre.

THE GATEKEEPER: The very same.

THE PETITIONER: For a bishop's head or... the mitre of a woman?

THE GATEKEEPER: Of a woman!

THE PETITIONER: Then, it is OK. It is still a Gate!

THE GATEKEEPER: You are right it is still a gate! And it is also holy, it's all you could do... it will do... We haven't got any frankincense!

THE PETITIONER: Have you brought wormwood and wild thyme? Burn them. *(He kneels down).* While you were away, the Gate has grown again. *(He crosses himself with pagan gestures)*

THE GATEKEEPER: It is a good sign... Help us holy Gate, open to us a way in life and in death, make it easy for us, show us the way onto eternal happiness and good, Gate to the Temple, Gate to the House, Gate to the Soul, Gate to Success, Gate to Heaven, Gate to the Good ones, and then, when we don't try you according to the rules, Gate of Hell... Amen!"

THE PETITIONER: Amen. *(With his forehead, he bends to the ground)*

(The Gatekeeper strokes his back with affection, then he suddenly rises, he pulls the cable of the lantern, he stealthily comes closer to The Petitioner, he throws himself onto him, trying to tie him down)

THE PETITIONER: I say, what are you up to? Let me go. *(On his belly):* Are you trying to get revenge on me? *(He returns under the Gate)* I hit you on the head with the bench out of... a polemic spirit! *(He fights)* It has been a simple contradictory discussion! *(The Gatekeeper uses any position to tie him down)* I don't like it! You vile man, I am not one of those. *(The Gatekeeper has tied his* *hands; he fastens them to the root of a bush. He goes on to do the same to his legs: he ties them to other bushes and roots one at a time)*

THE PETITIONER: I am a virgin, you monster, and... I have haemorrhoids!

THE GATEKEEPER: But you have a clean soul.

THE PETITIONER: You are completely mad! Oh Lord, save me: I am content with what I have!...

THE GATEKEEPER: Well, well, you are the right person!

THE PETITIONER *(He is sobbing)*: I am young, man, what do you want to do to me? Why? I don't understand!... *(The Gatekeeper is staring inquisitively)* Talk, mister, are you a sadist?... My hands are aching, and I have got a thorn in my foot!...

THE GATEKEEPER: I am looking at you for the greatest event of all. I envy you! If **you** could do to me what I am preparing to do to you, I would exchange our roles on the spot. You wouldn't even need to tie me down. You are a happy man, and I envy you...!

THE PETITIONER: Let's exchange places! Free me! I promise to do to you whatever you want!...

THE GATEKEEPER: You cannot. You have not got enough strength.

THE PETITIONER: How do you know it? *(In despair)* I love you. Untie me!

THE GATEKEEPER: Your desire is not ripe enough and, deep down, you still believe it to be wrong. You are not prepared to do this yet.

THE PETITIONER: But I am: after three months of isolation in a training camp, all soldiers looked beautiful, slender, warm, and they smelt maddening...!

THE GATEKEEPER: You are too young...

THE PETITIONER: I don't like women! *(In despair):* I like only men: they are robust and they smell pleasant! Even if they do not shower...!

40

THE GATEKEEPER: ...And you are a liar, too. *(Suddenly)* Why did you hit me on the head with the bench?

THE PETITIONER: I? Never! I lied to you!

THE GATEKEEPER: Therefore, then...I was noy asleep, as I believed initially. You hit me in the head and I fainted! You put me to sleep like an animal, at the abattoir. Then you excited me. You stroked me while I fainted... You raped me! Tell me the truth!

THE PETITIONER: I was under the impression that you have killed yourself. I wanted to administer first aid to you!

THE GATEKEEPER *(Ironically):* And you administered it to me...! Are you satisfied?

THE PETITIONER: It wasn't what you think. Or what you might believe!

THE GATEKEEPER: May the Lord forgive you!

THE PETITIONER: I utter the truth. You are committing an awful sin! Will you kill me?

THE GATEKEEPER: First, I shall clean you.

(He walks to the support on the left of the Gate; he turns with a bottle of water from the shade and with a packet of cotton wool. He tears bits of cotton wool from his packet, he soaks them in the liquid, and he wipes The Petitioner's face and hands)

THE PETITIONER: I am washed, pig. When you are in front of the Gate, you are getting ready! I am not insensitive...!

THE GATEKEEPER: You have sweated with worry.

THE PETITIONER: But I have not sweated.

THE GATEKEEPER: You smell bad, of musk. Have you peed on yourself, or you haven't washed your armpits!

41

THE PETITIONER: I should have smashed your skull, beefy pervert!

THE GATEKEEPER: I am disgusted by how you smell, that's all; I have nothing to do with you.

THE PETITIONER: If you are trying something, I shall pee on myself!

THE GATEKEEPER: It would be a pity.

THE PETITIONER: On my word! Let me see: how are you going to proceed then? *(He laughs hysterically).* How will you do it?... (Roars of laughter)

THE PETITIONER: Can't you say something nice? Something sensitive? *(He draws out some scented serviettes from his chest; he wipes his neck and behind his ears).* We are talking about your last moments on Earth.

THE PETITIONER: Without the vicious perfume of dung. Rotten sausage!

THE GATEKEEPER: Please, I want you to like the idea. I want you to be really happy. ...Can you sing?

THE PETITIONER: I've got it! I've got it! Why don't you masturbate?

THE GATEKEEPER: You use un-educated language. Very bad!... You haven't been educated when you were little, very little...! Poor you!...

THE PETITIONER: Have your parents caught you masturbating in the bathroom? Have they caught you? Tell me. Have they caught you? Tell me!

THE GATEKEEPER: No.

THE PETITIONER: Have you seen what a suitable place it is? *(He laughs in despair).* Untie me!... *(Sobbing)*

THE GATEKEEPER: This is your destiny.

THE PETITIONER *(He screams):* Why don't you go into the bushes? Let's play father and son. I am the father, you are the son, and the brunches are the bathroom. You calm down and... let me go. Please!...

(He is crying. The Gatekeeper tidies up his clothes, he crosses himself in front of the altar, he kisses "the icon", and he dances ritualistically. Then)

THE GATEKEEPER: You helped me build a beautiful altar. Help me to God! I shall put a tuft of your hair at the icon. Into eternal memory.

THE PETITIONER: First you rape me, and then you kill me.

THE GATEKEEPER *(Amazed):* I did not rape you, I don't like men: I worship you!

THE PETITIONER *(Amazed):* What, that is to say?! And you, half-witted sadist, have you made so many preparations only to kill me?!

THE GATEKEEPER: I shan't kill you dear! I shall sacrifice you! Then, I shall burn you complitely in the honour of the icon that you made. You offended me terribly...!

THE PETITIONER: Has It asked? Has the Gate asked for this?

THE GATEKEEPER: The Gate does not ask: we must show respect. I wish to show my respect to It, and to your work, and to Its Icon. Thus, I show respect to your talent too! You should be the first to fight for this holy cause, but you are far too conceited: do you really believe that you represent so much and that you desperately love this absolutely wretched life?

THE PETITIONER: Do the masters of the Gate know what you intend to do?

THE GATEKEEPER: They will learn at the right time. And they will agree.

THE PETITIONER: But, do they know? Is this their will? Has the Gate got any masters? Is it omnipotent, does it decide and judge everything? Does it judge alone?

THE GATEKEEPER: It has got a master. *(He is looking out at sea; the yacht is whirling in a circle).* It seems they are discontent. I don't understand!?... I made a mistake somewhere...!

THE PETITIONER: Does it judge all by itself?

THE GATEKEEPER: Who?

THE PETITIONER: The Gate: has it got the power to judge all by itself, to make decisions and to apply them too?

THE GATEKEEPER: You disappoint me: the Gate is a symbol!

THE PETITIONER: Then, it is only an intermediary! One does not bring offerings to an intermediary! I know that for certain! Everyone is appointed for his loyalty. One hasn't got any other qualities. Do you realize what you are taking upon yourself?

THE GATEKEEPER: But a small altar, it is worth it! To show respect.

THE PETITIONER: This, yes.

(Quiet. The Gatekeeper looks in the distance)

THE GATEKEEPER: The yacht has stopped. It is waiting. Is it waiting for something? I see, I was wrong...

THE PETITIONER: A thorn has entered my foot. It is aching. Do something!

THE GATEKEEPER *(He strokes him on his cheek):* What an exquisite offering you would have been!...

THE PETITIONER: Damn it!

THE GATEKEEPER: You buzz all the time! *(He snatches his ties).* Do you know you have confused me? Maybe you are... even the devil himself.

THE PETITIONER *(He hits him in the chin with his fist).* For the fright you have given me.

THE GATEKEEPER *(from the ground):* You could have become a martyr; you have no idea what you have lost. You will regret later. How much you will regret!... Do you realize how many people would have worshipped you?

THE PETITIONER: If you tried to rape me, perverse and flagged frankfurter, I had a fart ready... I...

(They laugh, up to the point of fainting)

THE GATEKEEPER: A perverse and flagged frankfurter...! Ha, ha, ha!... Where do you find them?!... You really believe that I am...?

THE PETITIONER: And aren't you?

THE GATEKEEPER: I am not. It is nonsense!

THE PETITIONER: Maybe you don't realize because of prejudice, but a little, a very little, you must be, otherwise... Don't tell me that...! Damn those pigs: They mocked at us, we are both idiots, they tricked us! The Gate is only... an ordinary object!

(The Gate screeches, it opens slightly, and then a bit more, then it stops. The Petitioner pushes The Gatekeeper; he speeds away in an attempt to cross beyond. The Gate suddenly closes; it catches his right hand between its folds. The Gatekeeper rushes towards The Petitioner who is screaming in pain)

THE GATEKEEPER: You mean person! Do you scream? Did you want to trick me again? Let me give you a good reason to scream! *(He hits him between the legs. The Petitioner falls on his knees)* Haven't I kept on telling you that you have no business here without my permission? *(He hits him skilfully).* You never listen! You like to drive people out of their senses! And you enjoy being beaten! You masochist! That's for you, villain! Bad lot! Good-for-nothing! Double-dealer! Are you trying to pull wool over my eyes? You wreck! *(He hits him revengefully)* Are you trying to waste my strength little by little? You have succeeded! *(He hits him).* Water is pouring off me.

(Mother shows herself)

MOTHER: How are you feeling, my darling?

THE PETITIONER: Well, MOTHER. I couldn't be better.

MOTHER: Your habit to self-banter.

THE PETITIONER: No, I am well. And you? How are you? Father?

MOTHER: He is also well. We have decided. We discussed a lot and we have decided.

THE PETITIONER: Are you moving out? I have been asking you for the past two years now. Life is beautiful on the farm - hens, rabbits, quails, pigs, peacocks, but, it's true, it is dirty, vulgar, I have told you: it is not for old intellectuals like you. It is for the young ones. Mainly for those without any prospects.

MOTHER: You are rushing it as usual, my darling. We have decided: we are moving beyond. We are leaving for good.

THE PETITIONER *(not understanding, surprised):* Where?

MOTHER: From where we all came.

THE PETITIONER: What on Earth are you talking about, MOTHER?

MOTHER: We have had enough, my darling: it has become boring here. And we have little to do... and our pensions are hardly sufficient... It is too degrading for us.

THE PETITIONER: Mother, if I have been at fault with something...

46

THE GATEKEEPER: When you follow your destiny, you are not at fault. You are not in the wrong, my darling. This is how you are, this is your destiny, and why do you want to be in the wrong?

THE PETITIONER: Do you want... Have you spoken to anyone? Who has put all these stupid ideas into your head? I want to know him! I want to talk, I want to talk to him!...

MOTHER: My darling, father has convinced me, I have convinced father... Do you wish to punish us?

THE PETITIONER: Mother, I don't understand!

MOTHER: Carla has disappeared... She was the only being who was making us still feel useful. We have received a letter from her, from Brazil - she is not coming back. You can find her letter on the nighttable, near the telephone, which we have cancelled. Don't worry: you will pay nothing when we've gone. I cancelled the TV subscription and the gas; from the selling of the car I paid the mortgage on the flat and signed a contract, - you will find it next to CARLA's letter -, with an undertaking firm...

THE PETITIONER: Mother...!

MOTHER: There will be no problems - the money ones are excluded, I made sure of that. We... we'll crash against the pavement, and that's all! We'll make a bit of a mess, but you put Stelică...

THE PETITIONER *(He screams)*: Mother!

MOTHER: Father and I, we have never flown. It was the only thing we wished for. Now... we'll do it. Please be happy for us.

THE PETITIONER: Mother, I beg of you, please forgive me if I have wronged you. I believe that I have wronged you, don't leave me on my own...!

47

MOTHER: Farewell my darling. There is so much boredom here… Father and I, we are leaving… We'll see each other again. (*She disappears*)

THE PETITIONER: Do not leave me alone…!

THE GATEKEEPER (*He hits him*): You are special, aren't you? Who are you talking to? To your memories, aren't you? You are special, and you don't even utter a word when I hit you… (*He hits him*) self-sacrifice! Why do I sweat here for, animal? Why? (*He hits him*) Go on, scream! Scream, damn who has given birth to you, so that I can hear you. I want to hear how you scream. Ask for forgiveness, you good for nothing! (*He hits him*)

THE PETITIONER (*He screams*): The Gate has caught my hand! Look! It has crushed my fingers!

THE GAMEKEEPER: If you never listen…! (*Suddenly, worried*): Pull, this is no good: Pull, I shall be punished!

THE PETITIONER: It's draining me!

THE GATEKEEPER: Gently pull.

THE PETITIONER: I have bony joints; they don't squeeze through the opening, do something!

THE GATEKEEPER: The alarm was not activated. (*He looks into the horizon through the metal bars*) No… It has not been activated. (*He pulls the Gate*)

THE PETITIONER: Do not jerk it because it will crush my bones! Bring a crowbar.

THE GATEKEEPER: All the iron from this beach has been incorporated into the Gate.

THE PETITIONER: A wooden lever.

THE GATEKEEPER: All the big objects that could have been used as weapons had been incorporated in It. The wood was burnt in the blast furnace.

THE PETITIONER: O…!

THE GATEKEEPER: And the stones: they had been buried into its foundation. They support it so that it does not fall… I cannot do anything… Why are you putting me in situations without issue? *(He is crying)* I am losing you...! We were almost getting on with one another!...

THE PETITIONER: I don't feel the pain any longer. In exchange... I am feeling awfully sleepy.

THE GATEKEEPER: This comes from the pain! Oh Lord, what shall I do?

THE PETITIONER: I am fainting...!

THE GATEKEEPER: If you collapse, you'll break your arm! Stand up!... Can you draw with your left hand? Can you?

THE PETITIONER: Bring a bench to hold on.

THE GATEKEEPER: We desecrate the altar!

THE PETITIONER: You can't... *(He slides on his knees)* Holy... holy passing, gate named... *(He slides down)*

THE GATEKEEPER: Control yourself! *(He catches him)*

THE PETITIONER: Thanks. But it was no loss: I was breaking my arm, which will not be of any use to me anyway: The Gate has crushed my fingers.

(The Gatekeeper puts his left arm on his shoulder; he supports him while looking around in despair)

THE GATEKEEPER: If you annul precisely what makes you special, the gift of drawing, all will be lost!

THE PETITIONER: What a pleasant warmth is burning my fingers!... It is like warm milk!... It is warm cream!... Let me... I can support myself... *(He falls asleep)*.

THE GATEKEEPER *(He screams):* It's not fair!... Why did you want to run away? Surely I wasn't menacing you in anyway. We felt good in each other's company *(He cries in despair)*. Both of us could have done so much...! You were somebody on this beach... It's not fair!...

(The Gate opens suddenly; both of them fall onto the soil. Silence. After a while)

THE PETITIONER *(He wakes up, he ascertains):* He has understood at last! Your Gate is kind... *(To The Gatekeeper)* I have heard everything you said. And It has heard us. Due to you It has forgiven me.

THE GATEKEEPER: It has agreed that's all. It means that you are on a good path, the happy one!

THE PETITIONER: This happiness smells bad to me.

THE GATEKEEPER: You are cursing.

THE PETITIONER: I am ascertaining.

THE GATEKEEPER: You are blaspheming.

THE PETITIONER: I feel it!

THE GAMEKEEPER: In this case, I do not respect you any longer!

THE PETITIONER: After It crushed my fingers, after you hit me like a horse-thief, can my happiness stink of roses?

THE GATEKEEPER: I was beating you for your own good!

THE PETITIONER: Too much art, too much killing and only out of pure love!

THE GATEKEEPER: You didn't want me to make a fool of myself in front of... The cad you are: I am a professional, you brick, what on earth!?

THE PETITIONER: You exaggerate, little man.

THE GATEKEEPER: Didn't you like when I stopped hitting you? And when the Gate let hold of your hand, wasn't it wonderful?

THE PETITIONER *(Ironic):* Most of all, these are the moments I enjoyed the most: when I rid myself of the sensation I was going to excrete.

THE GATEKEEPER *(learned):* The pleasure is in the struggle of returning with benefit from the path towards death! With each pleasure we die a little. *(Suddenly)* Which is the most beautiful death towards which you got the closest and, as a result of which, you remained alive enjoying great satisfactions?

THE PETITIONER: Now, that we went through so many things together, will you allow me beyond?

THE GATEKEEPER: You don't wish it.

THE PETITIONER: But I wish to pass!

THE GATEKEEPER: Will you listen to what I am saying!

THE PETITIONER: Damn it, your fixed ideas with sexual connotations annoy me!

THE GATEKEEPER: Hah, hah, have you got it? As many orifices as many possible deaths, and an equal number of pleasures exist. Mathematically!

THE PETITIONER: But the drugs in the vein?

THE GATEKEEPER: If you shut down a man's orifice for ever, just a single orifice, if you shut down a single poor hole in his body for ever: he dies! On the contrary, if you shut it down delicately, then you open it, then you shut it down, then you open it again, and so on and so forth, the man feels how it comes, how it comes through his veins, moist, hot and soft, for you are weaning him from his death, rhythmically and he feels how deep pleasure... floods him...! Pleasure sleeps close to death, and unfortunately it is the one who wakes up!

THE PETITIONER: You are mad.

THE GATEKEEPER: Look... the kiss! Think! Or... eating and drinking: Close... open... close... open, what about that? The mouth: chomp-chomp, chomp-chomp, chomp-chomp... Well? The belly swells, the veins dilate, the eyes open wide, the blood circulates... Well?

THE PETITIONER: If I tell you that I understand, will you let me be? Move aside. I understand.

THE GATEKEEPER: I have never got so far with anybody else...! *(He yells exultantly)* lu, huuu!

THE PETITIONER: Yes, without a shadow of a doubt: you are mad!

THE GATEKEEPER: I am happy.

THE PETITIONER: I let you take your fling, but help me…! Hello, just listen to yourself! I say can you hear me?

THE GATEKEEPER: As a matter of fact, pleasure is a rhythmic game with death.

(The Gate screeches, it opens a little. To The Gatekeeper's surprise, The Petitioner walks, not towards its opening, but to its support)

THE GATEKEEPER: Back.

THE PETITIONER: I want to oil it.

THE GAMEKEEPER: Do you want to oblige me?

THE PETITIONER: I only wish to oil the Gate.

THE GATEKEEPER: Why?

THE PETITIONER: Because it cries.

THE GATEKEEPER: It screeches.

THE PETITIONER: It cries1

THE GATEKEEPER: But what the damn have you got with its crying? It is my mission to take care of its screeching.

THE PETITIONER: I wish to oil it. And don't swear at me.

THE GATEKEEPER: Do you want to get something?

THE PETITIONER: Your shortcoming is that you are suspicious and brutal.

THE GATEKEEPER: And what are you going to oil it with?

THE PETITIONER: With my blood. I have filled in my fists, and I have enough.

THE GATEKEEPER *(He screams)*: Back *(To himself)* …I don't know what I am supposed to do in this situation… What am I to do?

THE PETITIONER: Easy: you allow me to oil the Gate *(He oils the hinges of the Gate)*

(Celestial music can be heard. The Gate opens slightly. From the horizon, the yacht floats towards It, it grows, it grows enormously, it covers the whole beach, and it is, alas, a fairytale castle. THE MESSENGER walks down the steps of the castle. It goes through the opening of the Gate; he carries an immense postman's bag on his shoulder. He stops in front of the terrified Gatekeeper)

THE GATEKEEPER: This has never happened to me!... Never...

THE PETITIONER: Don't be scared. You are dreaming.

THE GATEKEEPER: On the contrary, it is true!

THE PETITIONER: You are dreaming it is true.

THE GATEKEEPER: Is it true that I am dreaming?...

THE MESSENGER: Are you The Gatekeeper?

THE GATEKEEPER: I am! He is a petitioner. Very persuasive and tenacious. *(Trembling with fear)* In my opinion, he can go through!

THE MESSENGER *(He takes a correspondence notebook out)* Sign it!

THE GATEKEEPER *(terrified)*: But I have consciously done my duties! Why should I sign?

THE PETITIONER: Sign it. Anyway, it has been decided.

THE MESSENGER: You question an order. Have you got any explanations?

THE GATEKEEPER *(Trembling)* I don't question any order, but I have got the right to know why...!

THE MESSENGER *(He takes an envelope out, he hands it to him)*: For this.

(The Gatekeeper signs, and trembling, he opens the enormous envelope, he reads it, he falls on his knees, he

bursts into laughter, his emotion turns into bursts of crying, he walks on his four limbs, he drags himself onto the steps of the Castle, he enters)

THE PETITIONER: Haven't you got a letter for me?

THE MESSENGER: What is your occupation?

THE PETITIONER: I am an artist… Fifteen exhibitions…!

THE MESSENGER: Talented?

THE PETITIONER: Until the public got to know me very well, my confrères maintained that I was not. After I began to be successful, my confrères began to deny it, and my friends became my enemies' friends.

THE MESSENGER: Are you alone? Fifteen exhibitions and you are still feeling alone?

THE PETITIONER: This does not bother me very much.

THE MESSENGER: Are you discontent?

THE PETITIONER: The fact that they are satisfied that they have isolated me, saddens me. They don't know that they forced me to get to know myself and develop further. And in a good way!

THE MESSENGER: You came here to cross beyond.

THE PETITIONER: Yes.

THE MESSENGER: You fought.

THE PETITIONER: I would like to cross.

THE MESSENGER: Your time hasn't come yet.

THE PETITIONER: I have always been patient. What was written inside The Gatekeeper's envelope?

THE MESSENGER: Nobody knows what is written inside one's last envelope.

THE PETITIONER: I beg your pardon for I am a bit indiscrete.

THE MESSENGER: You said the right thing. Are you staying?

THE PETITIONER: If it has been decided…!

THE MESSENGER: Yes.

THE PETITIONER: Then, I am allowed to stay.

THE MESSENGER: Do you know it all?

THE PETITIONER: I believe I do.

THE MESSENGER: I shall return, when it is necessary.

(The Messenger goes through the open gates, which close in the sound of iron. The Messenger climbs the stairs, the Castle moves away, it turns into a yacht and it covers the horizon to the left of the sea.)
The new Gatekeeper picks up the former Gatekeeper's cap, places it on his head, he moves the benches nearer the supports of the Gate, - and he resets the initial setting. A Petitioner enters)

THE PETITIONER: Good day.

THE GATEKEEPER: I was just forced to fracture my dearest dream…

THE PETITIONER: Greetings.

THE GATEKEEPER: I am forced to pretend I am pleased!

THE PETITIONER: I am busy. *(He points beyond the Gate)*

THE GATEKEEPER: And I don't know if I have the strength to play this imposed play…! What do you want?

THE PETITIONER: I said only "good day".

THE GATEKEEPER: Maybe, for you, it's valid that the day is good, but as far as I am concerned, I am not interested in subjective statements!

THE PETITIONER: I have not stated such a thing!

THE GATEKEEPER: But what did you do?

(Johanna, with her eyes stuck in the distance, is crossing the beach in her electric wheelchair)

THE PETITIONER: I foretold it! That's it, I wished for it.

THE GATEKEEPER: I hate! *(Surprised)* I begin to hate…
I didn't wish for this. I was dreaming of something
totally different *(He shouts to Johanna)* And it is not true
that I worship my executioners!... I… am waiting! I
know how to wait… That's who I am!

THE CURTAIN

YOU ARE JUST A BODY
(Tu nu eşti trupul tău !)[2]

Characters:

He - has been released from gaol;
She - is doing overtime - cleaning.

*Near the doors of the performance hall, on an upholstered bench, **He** sleeps, dressed in old clothes, in the style that was in fashion in 1977. He is resting his head on a dark violet shirt, wrapped in a bundle, of doubtful cleanliness.*

He is restless, he sighs in his sleep, he is trying to say something, and he does not succeed. He holds his knees tight to his mouth; his extremely well polished pointed shoes are visible.

---

[2] **Printed in the volumes:** *„Căderea"*, Publishing House Gama, Iaşi, 1993; *„Jocuri (de unu, de doi...)"*, Publishing House Junimea, Iaşi, 1998; *„Doamne, fă ca Schnauzer să câştige!"*, Publishing House Casa scriitorilor, Bacău, 2004.
Performed at: Dramatic Theatre „Bacovia", Bacău, theatrical season 1993-1994, with the variant title: *„Te urăsc, iubitule!"*, director Dan Alecsandrescu; TVR National Theatre, 1994, director Eugen Todoran; „Fantasio" Theatre, Constanţa, (original title), theatrical season 1999 - 2001, director Florin Zăncescu; Dramatic Theatre „Bacovia", Bacău, (original title), theatrical seasons 2003 – 2005, director Florin Zăncescu.

Everything - his clothes, his gestures completed even in his sleep, the stubbornness with which he is clasping his belt of his empty grey rucksack - speaks of a strong personality.

A gong sounds the beginning of the show.

On the stage, composite scenery, a mixture of modern musical and Elizabethan theatre props.

In the wings, provincial advertisements for an "extraordinary" recital performed by Goj Galan (portrait etc. etc.).

She is sweeping, she is talking to herself, she is folding items made of cloth, etc.

She: They have left me alone to talk to myself. Like Moses in the wilderness! *(She is acting a past scene):* 'Good evening!' – 'Good evening!' – 'I shall finish this good evening by midnight...' – 'You'll manage it. Your children are already asleep... And your husband is at the canal. What could you do at home right now? Come back tomorrow! We must be present as from seven o'clock: Maitre Galan wishes to rehearse!' 'That's it. Couldn't I come earlier tomorrow morning?' 'No!'. I tried in vain! No one wants to understand me. Everyone is so selfish! They came back from the tour and they threw everything everywhere as if everything had fallen down from a loft. I must sort them out now! I must sort them out on categories: which one belongs to the theatre, which one belongs to the musical! Which one is from 'la-la', from 'la-la', which one is from the theatre, at the theatre... Because, if I mix them up, the king will administer justice on the stage with the trombone, and the one from the 'la-la' will blow into the sceptre tomorrow... I should really play a nasty trick upon them! They come and they utter a few words on the stage and then they moan 'Oh Lord, how much I work!...' And I work and I do not lament with 'Oh Lord, how my back aches!', all day long. If I were to consider it on its own merit... (*She is scared of a mouse. She screams terrified*) Ai! Ai! (*To herself*) The mouse does not reach here, because the piano has curved legs. And they are polished. Go away!... Go away, disgusting mange!... But I? How can I leave from here? Ai! Has it got scared? (*She turns on her knees and, from the top of the piano, she scrutinises the floor*) Mew! Listen, you? Mew! M, e, w! Mew! Do you understand? Are you going or aren't you?

(*She lifts the top of the piano and, still on her belly, she presses on the keys. He entered a few seconds ago. He is watching her with a mixture of curiosity and irritation*)

He: Hey! Fidget!

She: You startled me! Who are you?

He: What the devil are you doing on the piano?

She: (*pointing to the floor*) A mouse!...

He: And can't you make mice without shouting?

She: There is a mouse on the stage, Mister, don't be a swine!

He: You are twisting like a weathercock on the top of the piano and you woke me up only for this?

She: What do you mean by 'woke you up'?

He (*shouts*): Screaming! How do you think you woke me up?

She (*frightened*): But... you?... Where were you?

He: In the performance hall! I was asleep and I was happy!

She: What?!

He: Haven't you learnt that some people still have the bad habit of sleeping? To sleep, sleep! (*He snorts*) Do you understand? I'll go back to sleep, but... ssst! If you don't want me to climb up onto you!

(*He turns towards the entrance*)

She: Heeelp!...

He (*He steps towards her*): Do you understand what I said?

She: Do not move!

He: I told you to put the sound down!

She: Stay where you are, do you hear me? Stay because…!

He: Well I am standing here. Have you got sawdust in your head?

She: Where did you want to go?

He: To sleep. Are you nagging me?

She: Where… to sleep?

He: On the settee. Near the doors.

She (*terrified*): Alone?

He: Alone.

She: Heeelp! Hel… What are you doing?

He: I am going to unplug you.

She: Remain where you are!

He: Why on the devil are you shouting?

She: Because… I feel like it!

He: When you shout, I feel like I want to block your doorbell!

She: If you make another step, I shall not only shout, but I shall also scream.

He: I am running out of patience!

She: I shall not shout… If you sit down.

He: Look, I am sitting down. Is this OK? My Lord, what a bother…!

She: How long will it take you to reach me, if you… wished so?

He: Five seconds. If you were to torment me. Otherwise… you do not interest me.

She: Well, that's just the problem.

He: What do you mean? That I should be interested in you?

She: That is… that's it: that I cannot unlock the door at the back of the stage in five minutes.

He: So what, what's your hurry?

She: So that I can get away!

He: Away from me? (*he roars with laughter*)

She: (*she nods her head energetically*): Yes!...

He: I told you I am not impressed by you.

She: Until it suits you.

He: Shall we continue another time?

She: If you stand up, I'll stand up! I know what I have to do.

He: Rubbish has crossed your mind!

She: There is a window backstage. I shall reach it in four seconds and I shall go through the glass! I shall fall in the yard of the canteen. The people there... will catch you straightaway.

He: Are you mad? Have you thought that you can get me into trouble?

She: Why did you enter the theatre?

He: With one aim only: to sleep!

She: You will have to tell this to the police. You must tell me what you wanted to steal?

He: But, what precious items have you got here? What risk should I take to make you active again? I am referring to... such a noisy expression of your trust in your co-citizens' assistance. (*She bursts out laughing, stimulating him*) For example where do you keep, inside this wonderful and sumptuous quiet building, the gold and the diamonds that decorate your kings, princes and courtiers' costumes eaten by moths? Where are those treasures of gems, the rolls of rare cloth, the money, the Turkish money, the mahmudiye and the gold coins, the guldens and the rubbles, the filers and the marks, the halers and the levels, where, where do you hide them so well? (*She roars with laughter. He looks at her with curiosity, it amuses himself*)

We have not come to steal, because:

"...we are not from here, from there

We are precisely from Goleşti

61

Where you cannot find milk,
They take it away as soon as they milk it,
The cats at the crossing are crying,
Do not believe that you are poor,
Because we have forty-four vine props
Just on the hill at Mişelie
Of which the hare does not even know".

She (*laughing*): Please, please, do stop! It's enough...

He (*beats with his heels onto the floor, he dances slapping his shoes with his hands and he shouts*):

"The hand screams on the top of the boot,
Get the bow, the stretched bow,
The stretched bow, the ready bow.
It is ready to shoot the arrow.

     (*A pause. She roars with laughter. He starts again*)

Have I been given young to young,
Because they are fond of shooting
Over his mother's house
Against his mother-in-law's!..." (*He stops like a stone statue*)

She: I have asked you to stop, I am almost sick; I cannot laugh any more...

He: Are you a bit stupid?

She (*laughing*): I am. How might I not be if, instead of running away when I see a madman, I talk to him?

He: You mean you are dealing with a madman, aren't you?

She: You are! But mad people are dear to our Lord. (*She laughs*)

He: Do you believe this?

She: Well, I see how many he has created!

He: I'll climb onto the stage!

She: Go on. Oh Lord, something is happening to me at last...!

He: Aren't you afraid?

She: A bandit cannot speak like this. And no matter how... badly you are dressed... forgive me. If you want, you may return to the settee. I shall wake you up in the morning, so that the administrator cannot find you here. This one is capable of hiding all the lights from the loudspeakers and of saying that you stole them. Go then, because I shall be leaving shortly and I shall not disturb you any more.

He: I am not sleepy.

She: Now, I shall scream if you don't go!

He: Give me a rest. What place is this?

She (*laughs unsure*): You shouldn't try to convince me that you do not know where you are, because... You shouldn't repeat this, because I begin to be scared again!

He: Berbeni?

She: Your jokes are not funny...

He: The lorry dropped me right in front. I said to myself I should find a corner for shelter until tomorrow morning. I have some business to attend.

She: Bless you. The handlers did not find you because they were busy unloading the props. They were in a hurry. Shame on them for the manner in which they guard public property. Now, go.

He: I feel good here.

She: Go without fuss because I am busy. (*She is working*)

He: I had a dream.

She: 'Ram, pam, pam and I did not crack. When I cracked at ram, pam, pam!' ...Have you got it? Free. And see that I do not know how to read dreams.

He: But, if I talk, won't I interrupt you from your work!

She: At the buffet of the market tomorrow. There you can go thirteen to the dozen.

He: I have no chance: the pubs are full of blokes in search of listeners.

She: Well, I might want to speak to someone?

63

He: You can mind your own work. As a matter of fact, I don't need you to listen to me. It doesn't matter if you listen to me or not.

She: Mr, do you wish to confuse me? Go and sleep!

He: I got used to communicate with objects. I know how to talk even to a... spike! Take a door made of oak, which stubbornly remains there when one tries to pull it out with one's fingers and which one can hardly feel because of one's callosity. I spoke to it, I called for it, I implored it to come out, and I promised it to turn it into a knife, if it were to listen to me! But no, it stuck to its own opinion. It remained there, stuck! I touched its hinges with the blood from my smashed fingers... but it remained stubborn! It remained there. (*Up*) It will rust there, because I didn't have any help when I needed it!

She: OK, tell me. Well, tell me about your dream? Please!

He: Damn you.

She: Do not swear.

He: And what would you want? That I kiss you?... Work. Work, why have you stopped? Do not stare at me because I shall get onto you and I shall speed you up. I say, damn you, what an imbecile I am! With whom am I quarrelling...? If you imagine that you are able to mock at me...!

She: Ssst!

He: Is someone coming?

She: Be calm!... I only wanted to send you to bed. That's all. Why do we have to quarrel for this?

He: I told you that I feel good here!

She: Excellent! Then, stay. (*She is working*) What a lot of palaver for nothing!

(*Pause*)

He: A scarf has fallen behind the throne.

She: Thank you.

He: Some people must also work during the night and others...!

She: They were on tour. They have rehearsals with the master in the morning (*She is pointing to the advertisements on the boards*). They'll arrive at the theatre early in the morning. I finish my work here now and tomorrow... I shall arrive later.

He: Has he been working here for long?

She: Who?

He: 'The Master'!

She: He got a transfer this theatrical season. Do you know him?

He: I? Where from?

She: It seemed to me that you asked about him as if he were an acquaintance. Those who know him from the past say that he is very good.

He: Actors disgust me: the ant gathers and the grasshopper sings.

She: You are all skilled.

He: Well, well, I've exaggerated...

She: I mean you utter nonsense. But, regarding him, - he is very conceited.

He: Damn him... What does your family say when you do overtime in the evening? Or you don't do any.

She: But I do. My children are asleep; my husband is at the Canal... What could I do?

He: Two children?

She: Three.

He: Bless them. I... I am not married. The situation!

She: I imagined it.

He: I wanted you to understand that: 'not that I didn't want it!' The situation was that... it was not possible!

She: Yes, it is difficult to go with someone to the town hall!...

65

He: Do not take it this way. I couldn't because... I was rejected. They threw us like a bell clapper: from here to there. I couldn't grow roots like a tree does. Or like a man does with a woman...

She: Well! There are trees that root even in pails. One can move them from *here* to *there*, and if they wish, they can even produce fruit. And I have one at home: a ficus! I keep it on the balcony. It has fresh air, what else does it need? It turns green as if it were in its own soil.

He (*outburst*): There, when I was asleep on the banquette near the door, I felt that those who walked past me hated me.

She: One doesn't care a fiddlestick of what happens in a dream!

He: If you are normal! But if you know that the dream is a synthesis? The pure alcohol made from the husks of life? The dream is a fracture in existence, where the sight, the smell, the hearing and the thought - sometimes - cannot even reach!

She (*ironical*): As a career, you are a teacher of Chinese.

He: *I knew* I was asleep! *I was conscious* that I was asleep. *I could see myself* on that banquette: unshaven, with my clothes torn and crumpled, my knees under my chin, one hand wrapped up in the straps of the rucksack and with polished shoes. Well polished, accusingly bright and disgusted in the feet of a tramp. Out of fashion shoes, but brand-new. What a horror!... Like lifting a skirt in public.

She: Your shoes are very chic: "retro" is fashionable.

He: They were casting a quick scornful glance at me; I was grasping it with my third eye... - With my third eye, the one that reads thoughts! Upper class people, 'the cream', people with 'preoccupations'... I was asleep and I was feeling like a toothpick floating in milk.

She: Have you eaten anything today?

He: I wandered on without stopping. I haven't got... the time.

She: When did you come out?

He: The day before yesterday. How did you know?

She: Well I never, as if it were difficult. Where will you go?

He: I shall make... a little detour.

She: If you come out of 'there', the best will be if you go home first.

He: And you my dear, will you allow me to think for myself what I must do?

She: I do not interfere; you do what you want and what you believe to be right. Only that, I was thinking that... the detour is always risky, because... It always depends.

He: I give you my word that it depends on me only.

She: You are wrong. It depends *when* you do it and *where* you do it. Not to mention *your purpose*.

He: Really, what a lucky find!... An educated woman. The high school?

She: With awards! If this prevents you from falling asleep.

He: It keeps me awake, it keeps me awake, and, of course, it keeps me awake. But what do you have in mind?

She: It is normal to go home first.

He: Tell me the truth: do you wish to adopt me.

She: Don't be stupid. I am trying to make you understand that you have 'a label'!

He: Is there someone paying you to bother me?

She: If you wear 'a label', you are not worth a penny. You are allowed to do only normal things. And it is normal to go home first of all.

He: Have I invited you to come into my life? I don't remember. Why do you interfere?

She: Because I feel like it. Because I lived and because I live... What I said, I also said on my behalf. Do you understand?... It is difficult!...

He (*climbs onto the stage!*): I haven't told you anything. I invite you not to mix me up into your fantasies. You have been preaching to deaf ears!... Finish quickly what you must finish and leave.

She: I hit the nail on the head, man. If I haven't succeeded, you were to return to the hall to continue your sleep. Or you would have left. You didn't come here to talk.

He (*rude*): What on earth to talk about? What... Have I got anything in common with you? Have I lived like you? Do you wish for an exchange?

She: All right, good, that's it: I have finished! It cannot be, it cannot be like this!

He: But, of course that it cannot be like this!

(A pause)

She: ...It is very hot tonight! - I'd like to be silent. Perhaps you would feel better, but I cannot calm myself. I believe that the perfume and the quietness and the anticipation of the audience... You see, when the audience does not applaud, they talk and... when they do not talk, they applaud. - It hasn't rained for a while. The edges of the leaves have started to turn and the hares have entered the woods. The old people say that this is 'a sign'. Has it rained where you come from? - I am talking nonsense...

(She resumes her work)

He: Someone must supervise you... to check if you do what you are supposed to do... they wouldn't bet you are... so clever. How did you manage to get here?

She: Following a long road. And... with diversions!

He: It must be difficult for you.

She: Not as difficult as you might imagine. The production boss says that if one wants to be happy according to the new scientific targets, one must be content with what one has! (*She laughs*)

He: Your production boss is a bit of a cretin.

She: Why? He jokes. 'He synthesises the opinion', so he advocates it. It is funny! My husband has an ulcer with a niche. Due to stress. Every time when I ask for leave to take him food to the hospital, the boss lets me go: 'your husband's illness is a lot of fuss and nonsense! Instead of having an ulcer based on bacon and regional wine, he has it on alien bases. Hear me: stress!?... You cosmopolitans!' (*She roars with laughter*) Then see fun at the theatre. All gather round me, and then, allegedly, they side with me - I feel great: I have the sensation that I mean something to... them. We become closer, the hierarchy disappears, and we become closer... It is strange, but, sometimes, I waited and I wished that the boss mocked at me: 'hey, how is your American? Hasn't he decided to procure himself one of our illnesses, a healthy version?'... I like when he reprimands me - seriously or jokingly! - It's not a matter of masochism. He makes those around him notice me, analyse me... Due to him I made many friends. He is useful.

He: He is mean. I realise what you are saying.

She: And the medicine is bitter.

He: Mind you don't...?

She: Don't speak nonsense. He is sixty-two years old.

He: He gets on my nerves.

She: Mind your nerves and no one will get on your nerves.

He: I do not wish to annoy you.

She: OK. You convinced me that everything you do ends up badly just when you wish it to succeed!

He: I am delaying you!

She: To reach to your height!

He (*burst into laughter*): I do not believe that there are any amateurs left in town to rub you the wrong way.

She: That's why I was so eager for you to arrive.

(They laugh, in high spirits)

He: What's your husband's job... there?
She: At the Canal?
He: Yes.
She: He is clocking. At I.T.A. - auto transport!
He: Is he OK?
She: He maintains he has wonderful conditions: sleep, - free of charge, canteen, - low price, holidays, - in hospital!... All in all, he says, with minimal spending. He will return on state money when he gets better. He is very content. He is really, really content! (*Bewildered*) The end. Inventory. It has closed! (*Pause*) On Sunday, the children and I... listen to the radio... to the program... 'From the country's construction sites'. Solemn music, dynamic, 'we are breaking the mountains with our feasts!'... Then, we follow what they say it is happening over there. From where it is broadcast live! The day they talk about our construction site, where my husband works...! we celebrate after we listen to it. We go to the cinema; we walk in the park...
He: You have a full life.
She: I don't complain (*She giggles*) But you, when you are not... at...! 'the pension', what do you do?
He: You are direct.
She (*indifferent*): Damn them!

(They burst out laughing)

He: You have a screw loose!
She: Let it be.
He: I am glad that you woke me up...!

She: By the way: bear in mind that this declaration of a certain kind... irritates me. And so on and so forth.

He: Professionally, I am an economist. I was working for a vegetable farm. Until! When the inquiry happened...

She: Enough. I understand: you are a plumber. High school or apprenticeship?

He: You do not believe me.

She: but I do... I have read that, in our inner soul, every one of us is what one wishes to be. Only that I asked you what you do outside, in society that is.

He: A teacher. At the high school. I did it at night school.

She: Therefore... a waiter! It is not a bad job. I also wish to ask for a transfer. To the restaurant opposite. It is a living!

He: Are you put out that I am also a teacher?

She: You are not. You are not patient enough. You lack calm and your obedience has deserted you a long time ago. So there is... something else!

He: A lawyer! Well? What about that?

She: By all means, if that is agreeable to me? Tell me the truth, if you can. If not, not and... things being as they are! I shall not bring this up again.

He: I know the penal code. I studied at the Faculty of Law in Iaşi!

She: The Faculty?

He: Yes.

She: The Faculty with or without stripes on the clothes?

He: Aren't you tired of going on and on?

She: What can I understand from what you are going on? What must I believe?

He: That I am a lawyer.

She: Only if you ask me. You must know that I eyed you up and down. You do not wish to tell me what you busy yourself with, or you are ashamed of your job - it's your business. Order me to leave you in peace and put an end

71

to this. You are beating about the bush. You better say that your family has abandoned you and it is because of them that you are here.

He: Shut up! If you utter another word about them, I shall ring your neck!... They!... You should not mix them up in this rubbish, which concerns me only... in which I find myself only because of me, because... Oh, Lord, what the devil am I doing?... Forgive me...! (*She is visibly scared*) I have always believed that I shall overcome my gremlins if I scream. Do not take into account what I have just said. I do not feel anything from all I have said. Only that they... With my parents, you must be careful; otherwise, you can tell me anything. Anything, I shall not get annoyed.

She: Really, haven't you found another place where you could spend the night?

He: The only document I have on me is my discharge paper. They would not have allowed me at the hotel. I have scared you...

She: I am guilty. Why did I need to know about your job?

He: Well, didn't you? It was clear: you were facing a convict! Why did you need to also know... other details about him? When an object has got 'a label', you know precisely how it was made, why it was made and especially... you know how to use it. So that it does not electrocute you!

She: I did not know how to say this.

He: But you said that I had 'a label'.

She: When I said this to you, I believed you were cleverer.

He: Listen, do not bewilder me. - When 'shoes' is written on the box, you know that there are shoes inside it. When *it is written on me* that I am 'a convict', *you* know precisely that there is a convict inside. Well, madam, you are mistaken: There is a free man *inside me*! Nobody has succeeded or will ever succeed to chain me. I rise as much as I wish in myself, I have no obstacle and I climb down where I wish and I am disgusted of many more things than some might wish onto me - I do not give a damn! Neither my scorn can be censored by anybody, nor my love! So there, as you can see, I am a Man: you must show some *interest*!

She: My father in law advocates that a thinking mind damages one. (*He plays*) 'The money counts and not the mind!'

He: He might be a... good man.

She: He is. He has taken us out, my husband and I from the university entrance exam. He had learnt that we wished to 'do silly things' and he came after us. 'I say, our lot have always been honest. No one has been an intellectual: all were left with their biography creased and, in exchange, we had money! Pack your bags and... home. To work!' (*She laughs*) He convinced us.

He: An alcohol addict?

She: On the contrary.

He: A sectarian.

She: No, he only refused to help us with money during our university studies. 'I say, money is made; only advice is given. That's why I came after you: to advise you.'

He: And you?

She: I persisted in not divorcing. I haven't seen them for... ten years."

He (*strange*): You are longing... Isn't it true that, sometimes, you wish to ascend to heaven?

She: What's the matter with you?

He: Nothing, nothing... I wished only to learn... only... if you can bear not to see them.

She: It is as if... eh! - During the holidays, as they are teachers; they send someone to collect the children. They secure them summer camp tickets, or they keep them at their home... It is great!... I can save money and when I reckon that I have enough money, I begin to check the shops. It is something unusual, but you must know that it seems to me that... only then I can meet people. More precisely, only then I realise that I really meet them! Everybody asks me how I am, they tell me I am looking good, they ask me what I am going to buy... When I buy something, I choose for a long time, until I believe that I have found something that my mother or my father might like to buy for me, and... I buy it. I imagine that it is a present from them. Then I am very happy. I roam the streets... and... I am waiting. I am waiting for something to happen. This does not concern you. I cry in the evening. I cry a lot... Like a woman. That's it!

He: Will you divorce?

She: How have you invented this?

He: 'I take my children', 'I buy', 'I make...!'

She (*laughs*): I haven't got the time... And then my husband... He is a perfect flat mate: he is away most of the time, because he has work to do, he does not buy any clothes, because he wears those given by his firm, he stays in hospital free of charge...

He: And with the money? What does he do with the money?

She (*ironic*): Oh, because of it... he lives with a terrible guilt: he saves it at the bank. 'This will be my children's future!'...

He: It means that... you manage on your own!

She: Now it's OK. The middle one is walking; the little one will have his plaster cast taken out in a month time... - They fell from the balcony. Oh, what have I gone through...!

He: What about him?

She: When I came back from the hospital, I found him packing up his belongings. He said he was going to find some money. I asked him to stay on, because I had already sold the earrings given to me by my mother.

He: And?

She: And… he stayed on.

He: You! Don't you understand?...

She: But I do.

He: What are you doing for yourself?!

She: I don't even wish to think of it.

He: So that you live a lie!

She (*shouts*): A lie that helps me live!

(*Pause*)

He: You should know that I have been in prison… for attempted murder.

She (*dry laughter*): Do you wish to console me?

He (*acute tone*): It was a dirty trick, and I am not joking now!

She (*exhausted*): Good, I believe you.

He (*more acute*): A certain individual maintained that I spied on him and that, when he confronted me, I hit him in the head with a stone!

She: It must have been a pleasant moment.

He (*even higher pitch*): It was a dirty trick, don't mock at me! He called me! To suggest a dirty trick to me, that's why I hit him in his sticky mocking smirk!

She (*high pitch*): I believe you!

He (*even higher*): He lied only to get rid of me, to get me into trouble!

She (*idem*): I believe you!

He (*idem*): He put me in prison for nothing: he hit his temple on the stone when he fell! He lied…!

She: Enough!... I believe you, damn you lunatic! I believe you!

(*Pause*)

75

He (*irritated*): Why do you scream like this?

She: But you? What are you doing? Are you murmuring?

He: You did not believe me at first.

She: You were lying then.

He: And how do you know that I am not lying now? Because you noticed that this is my habit after all! Now, why not? What is your aim? Why don't you contradict me now?

She (*tired*): Don't you start again! Because now... you are conceited. After all I have told you, it would mean that you are much too mean to lie to me. You are part of those unfortunate individuals who are not insignificant...

He: I loved her immensely. The swine offered me money to give her up.

She: Calm yourself, I had enough.

He: When she walked passed you, you could feel that spring was in the air. She was bizarre. She had her own logic that tormented me. In her presence, I had the sensation that I was swimming in bottomless hot water, ready to absorb me at any time: I was in tears every time when I stretched my hands to hold her shoulders!...

She: You speak so beautifully about a woman...I must believe you!

He: Our paths crossed by chance. Once... I had just finished my second year at University, studying theatre, and she had finished the first year of her history course... I was accompanying her by train to Piatra - we were alone in the immense second-class carriage. At one station, three noisy individuals got on and suddenly started to throw paper balls. She pretended not to notice, but the vagabonds were chuckling amongst themselves, they were avoiding my eyes, pretending to be very interested in the fields which were unveiling passed us. I was feeling as if I were rabid. When I stood up, she stood up and she asked me to accompany her to the toilet. When we got there she pulled me inside. She blocked the door and she started to kiss me: 'Let them be, they do not count, you are the important one, you are brave, you are undaunted…!'

She: I believe you… She was extraordinary!...

He: She kissed me, she caressed me and I felt that she was charming me like one charms an apple, - with a raw taste - because there, in the piercing smell of disinfectant and urine, I had nothing of a man left in me. I was like a tree on which a wonderfully beautiful girl was climbing. My hate against the hooligans from the compartment was huge and it was growing in me, but not only that, I also burst into tears. She wiped my tears; I was unable to understand what was happening; she began to cry too. I screamed to be left alone. I burst into the compartment, I pulled the alarm cord, the train stopped and I demanded that those three individuals get off the train immediately in the middle of the field, to catch another train! Something happened, because those three individuals got off in great hurry. And I understood that I couldn't understand certain things, which, probably, are extraordinarily important.

She: You are utterly sincere!

He: When you hate yourself, you can afford to be sincere.

She: And, in your opinion, you are also very important.

He: I was trapped under the frame of the door two days and one night. My family was under the rubble, and… I knew. I knew!

She (*agitated*): You haven't talked about this, have you?

He: I thought that I might be able to tell you…

She: My thoughts are like water, if you empty the container, you carry it with more ease.

He: You dodge it… It does not matter. But, you know the reason far too well: you could have realized up to now that I cannot be only the container, I am also the water inside!...

77

She: Oh, Lord, how complicated you can be!...

He: The fact is that I was removed through a diabolical manoeuvre; the fact is that I was forbidden the being who I loved beyond everything else in the world: the fact that she let herself be tricked - could it have been with good reason? - Has it occurred to you that in all this, which could have muddled up even the mind of a tree stump, they were trying to make me feel basic?

She: I said 'complicated' in the sense that you muddle yourself up with all sorts of theories. Life is either in black or in white, hot or cold. Stop! It is neither lukewarm nor grey. Is it clear?

He (*stubborn*): She must learn the truth.

She: You must imagine how happy she'll be when she learns about it.

He: I imagine nothing: I believe that she knows exactly how things occurred.

She: What has gone down has gone down. When one missed the train, the only consolation is that one has the ticket. Do you wish to recover... the cost?

He: She must know!

She: But it is not right! You have arrived too late... It is as if you hated her... Everything has worked out. There is always sadness... left behind! Emptiness in emptiness... you get only an implosion of tears.

He: I do not know how to love anyone else!

She: And what was her fault? It is as if you were condemning her because she let herself be saved from drowning.

He: Nobody has saved her! Perhaps she might have believed it, but she wasn't saved: she was told lies!

She: And if the lies you told her made her happy?

He: It is not possible!...

She: Truth has never done anybody any good. Inhuman, monstrous, it cannot be mastered after it has been

78

uttered: it is perfect and cold like the insect of a nightmare.

He: How do you know it?

She: See how you shout? You are ready to claw me because you doubt it! How much perfume and how much beauty doubt is able to add to life, and how much monotony and how much boredom truth gives one...! Why are you so stubborn to shed light over misery?

He: Why do you put so much passion in what you say?

She: Because I wish to prevent you.

He: You are becoming extremely suspect.

She: Sometime, one could wait for something untrue, but which could lead one to something else other than suicide? Happiness, for example. I am not sure.

He: Do you know it all? Are you sure you are not missing something?

She: You are like the bee...! If no one happens to open the window, it hits the glass on and on. Poets also faint: alas, how much will come to light!... How much of the love of freedom!... Alas, how much more is left to us still to learn from nature!...

He: I am one of those who can tell you that the bee knows all too well what it does.

She: And I am one of those individuals with my head on my shoulders and I am telling you that, in fact, she is not able to find out!

He: You can be very bad... You said that doubt makes our life bearable. Even beautiful... Are you sure of what you are insinuating about me now?

She: Go home. Do not confuse people. Memories have no right over the present. I have also waited! And... I am like your history teacher: I couldn't bear if he showed up now... just now.

He: I believe you know whom I am talking about.

She: If you need, I can give you some money. Come back.

He (*stubborn*): I have enough money. I have worked there.
She: After all, it is your life. Can you help me?

(They arrange all sorts of things together)

He: And this?
She: Yes. There. (*Working, to her*) It is as if detention might have stopped your development. (*To him*) You behave like a teenager... Please forgive me! I shall not interfere any more.
He: Insist, insist, you have found me. (*Working*) Madness, you know how to nag me! You should have been a teacher.
She: I was! A supply teacher. At the five to eight years old. I was also a secretary, a typist and a season's labourer sorting fruit and vegetables... Everything: I have made my... 'contribution'. No one has any reason to complain about me. (*She laughs*) Only those who I struck when they tried to lure me into corners... In fact, this might be the explanation why... I changed so many work places.
He: You have squashed the initiative of those who wished to succeed by encircling you.
She: If I am stupid!...
He: It isn't chic! Better say disorientated!...
She: Do you know what mischief has crossed my mind?
He: But do you know what thoughts had crossed Ahmed al Ahmed's head, while he was spreading the prayer rug?
She: No!
He: A bullet... (*He laughs*)
She: Be serious!... I was thinking that we, all the women could start a common action: if we proceeded all together, but absolutely all of us, alike, in certain... situations, we could change the world in a very short time.

He: If all people were thinking alike, if they were feeling alike, if they were aiming for the same thing, - the world will be nothing but an ants-nest. Neither a madman nor an imbecile would wish to change us… into an ants-nest!

She: You are too serious… I am joking!…

He: Because of you: you have contaminated me. I must be the first case that demonstrates that wisdom is catching.

She: Stop it! I wanted to tell you how, sometimes, I amuse myself when memories overwhelm me.

He: Write an action plan for the offended women.

She: In three points! One: how an individual begins to moist his words in honey and pepper… March!

He: Ah!

She: Two: how, as soon as an individual has touched you… jart, hit him!

He: Oh…!

She: Three: how, when an individual tries to touch you where he shouldn't… trosc! Over the mouth.

He: Ouch!

She: And finished. In a couple of months, you sort out all the generations. (*She roars with laughter*) To the letter!

He: You are thinking like an old woman.

She (*parody*): But… I am suffering: because women do not accept my method.

He (*laughs*): Hypocrite…!

She (*laughs*): But I have acted alone: I was a missionary!

He: It seems that… you have been very active in - to express like this - the pedagogic field.

She (*idem*): Oho! I have educated very many men. From the moment they saw me… closer - I don't know what was wrong with them - they were overwhelmed by a wild desire… to learn their lesson!

He: I understand them. And…at the chapter of 'personal achievements'?

She (*guilty*): A bit… weak.

He: I see. From bad to worse! (*He points around.*) Un-pro-fit-able, citizen: unprofitable!

She (*idem*): You are right... Each spontaneous smack has cost me. An average... of about two hundred lei...

He: Official exchange?

She: Followed by scandal and transfer! Unofficial exchange, which is... adding what was applied in private, each smack makes much less: about ten lei!

He (*surprised*): How much?

She (*candid*): Ten-fifteen lei. The offer and demand law!

He (*idem*): O, ho, hooo!... You are a real entrepreneur!

She: I delivered to anybody, as much as one wished and at any given time.

He: I am not interested!

(*They burst out laughing*)

She: But, please!... I give it on credit.

(*They laugh with all their might*)

He: Shall I... touch you here?

She: Here!

He: Here...ha, ha, ha! On the shoulder?

She: Well! Just try it...!

He: You know, Madam: This very moment, I don't really *feel... like it*. I am missing this! Ha, ha, ha! I am missing it because of my fear!... I haven't laughed...!

She: Why don't you try? At least, try to find out how it is!

(*She walks towards Him*)

He (*withdraws*): Alas, Madam, I cannot afford... With my money... Well, no! No! No!... (*They laugh - they needed a relief from the whole issue. He puts his hand round her* *shoulders*). You madwoman!... You are mad. You are huge...! (*She sits down.*) That stupid man...! I don't know how he might be, but... What he has lost!...

She: Leave him alone...

(*Pause*)

He: I want to tell you something.

She: Don't you think it's time for me... to go?

He: If I don't tell you, I shall explode.

She (*smiling*): Watch it!

He (*is coming closer, he shows her his cheek*): You are welcome to hit me! (*Pause*) You are... beautiful...

She (*gazes at him*): Do not say this again! (*She turns away, she is working.*) You must not tell me. And... You are not allowed...!

He: But am I allowed to tell you that your place is not here, am I not?

She: I shall ask for a transfer to a restaurant.

He: And, you will finish like this: You have sorted your life out! You are not made for this. You are clever, beautiful and you have a sense of humour: you are young, - you can do anything! You have the right to wish for anything. What will you succeed with 'a transfer' to a restaurant... to a restaurant? What will you gain? Tell yourself now: to you and not to me!... Tell me: what will you achieve?

She (*high pitched and in tears*): Everything!... And damn you! What are you prodding at? I am happy. I am content. I am glad, look: I have tears of joy down my cheeks! Are you proud?... I am missing nothing! I need nothing! I have more than I need! I have you to bother me. Even my memories are in excess! (*She is crying calmly. Pause*)

83

He (*undecided*): As usual, it has turned out badly… I bring bad luck. It's high time for me to leave. (*He is leaving to the performance hall*)

She (*crying*): Damn you, stay put! It is not your fault!...

(*Pause*)

He: As a matter of fact, if you analyse it, the solution you are thinking of is good.

She: You know what? Rather than saying stupid things, be quiet!

(*Pause*)

He: I was picking a quarrel with you.

She: Do not waste your time! You were right.

He: Each time I am right, I feel like a swine!

She: And I… I feel like a squeezed lemon: very tired and… very clean; very tired and… very empty; very tired and… very sincere. You, can you be honest?

He: What has come onto you?

She: Do you know? What I already told you is rigmarole: that I wish for you to leave. As a matter of fact, I feel good here. Though… I do what you see me do…. I can hardly wait to see tomorrow's performance! Has he been your colleague?

He (*is startled*): Pardon?

She: Goj Galan. Were you at university together?

He: Which university are you talking about? 'The striped one'?

She: I guess that you are about the same age (*Doubting*). But perhaps…

He: I know of him indirectly. He had graduated when I began my course. He was talked about as being talented, but I heard that he 'manufactured' his successes by informing on his colleagues! A dirty dog!

She: He lives somehow secluded.

He: So, here too…!

She: Are you glad?

He: Why? If I knew him…!

She: However, he is considered to be very good… He plays in movies, he is on television…!

He: He is hardly at home.

She (*laughs*): Oh, not this, his wife accompanies him each time. When she asks for a holiday, it is known in town that Galan has a new contract. He does not lose sight of her. It is tragic what kind of love has touched poor them!

She: He has a certain way of imposing himself. The director listens to him religiously. No one dares crack any political jokes in his presence: they have put themselves out.

He: They are scared! The professor always compared what I was doing, with what… he was doing! (*Harsh*) And my professor said that I was much better than him! Much better!

She: I am not particularly keen to talk about him, you are getting wound up.

He: Forgive me!... I don't know what got into me to show off!?

She: I… even believe that you were better!

He: Words. Everyone is… what one is.

She: It means that you are back.

He: Where?

She: How, where?

He: To university?

She: Well, why?

He: With my police record?

She: Are you sure that you have cut all your bridges?

He: Perhaps I'll try. But first…!

She: 'This first' finished you off. You poor scatter brain!...

He: But you?

She: Why me?

He: You… them?

She: Why, 'them'?

He: You, what are you turning upside down here? You like it here, at the theatre, because you can look at *that one*! And… at others! How they play - good or bad. But you? How can you break the ice with everyone?

She: I just do it.

He (*irritated*): I d-o it! Perhaps the children. And you can still give lessons…! You, you do not even have the courage to dream. The cloth, the broom, sh, sh; the children, the plaster, the food, - splash, plash; your dishonest husband…!

She: Please!

He:…your miser husband!...

She: Do you know him?

He: Well: the miracle consort, - lulu, lulu!... And finished: the sleep!

She (*laughs*): What shall I dream of? When I dream, I dream either that a car hit the little one, or that the middle one fell from the nut tree…

He: See where you have got! I said that you were dreaming with your eyes wide open. Conscious. You should have this courage.

She: That is, I should think of what might be. I haven't got the time. Then, it is dangerous.

He: Have I told you that *dreaming* is what distinguishes animal from man?

She: The word!

He: The word is in the dream. All that man *imagines* has a name. *The word* is in the dream and the dream is the word!!!... If the dream didn't exist, we shouldn't exist either!

She: Sometimes I wished I were ill. I wished I were in hospital, quietly thinking. Of the many things I haven't got to think of...! It would be great. I tried, but... I did not succeed. Look: once I put the children into bed, I gave him his meal, I washed the dishes, I swept the kitchen, I prepared the lunches for the following day, I set the alarm to ring at four o'clock and I went onto the balcony. I intended to think! (*She laughs*). To experience what thinkers feel when they think... detached from the present!

He: Do you always go to bed so late?

She: I sat on the edge of the pail inside which I have a ficus, I took my head into my hands and... *'That's it, I said it to myself, I'll begin to think!'* But, as I was sitting like that and I was trying to think of something nice and concentrate upon it, I burst into tears. My Lord and what tears?!... My husband came to me. (*She laughs*) He thought that something had fallen on my foot! My children came too... They pulled me into the room, they asked me what was happening, and they asked me to calm down, because I had scared them, but I couldn't do it! I was crying, - look; even now I feel like crying. I cried without knowing why, and I told myself that it would be better if I threw myself over the balcony rather than try to think! I fell asleep crying and the following day when I got up he had left us. The children were at school... 'Here you are, I said to myself!'... Thoughts... bring trouble to those uninvited. (*She laughs sadly*) I am like a bride's veil over the bearded head of a priest.

He: You did not have the strength to detach yourself. One thing is to clod your girl's dreams in *the present situation*, and then, there is another thing to ennoble *the present situation*, with dreams of what you might do. Of what you might be!... Remember: you were happy then, a long time ago, because you had dreamt of being something else than what you are *now*! You will have to try again. You will have to try once again. And again...

She: It is not worth risking all for a moment of delusion.

He: Yes, it is! It's a must! It is worth it, if it weren't worth it, I would be already dead!

She: I know it is worth it, stop it, I am not a cretin, but every time I imagine one thing, something else becomes a reality. The result is always different, that's what I am afraid of!

He: I read somewhere that fear has a thousand feet. It is horrible that a thousand feet should ache each evening.

She: I have three children, a family. It is easy for you to be clever.

He: I do not understand the dream as a punishment! A kind of intoxication with cream.

He: A lot of cream is consumed where you come from.

He: You cannot imagine how much!... Sweet and coloured in many shades...

(*He begins to play a pantomime: field, wind, quietness, sun, insects, and flowers*)

She: What are you doing?

(*He does not answer her. She watches him puzzled. She understands. He offers her 'a flower'. She refuses. He insists. She stands up, catches 'the flower', she smells it, and she enters the game. A feeling of embarrassment invades her and she lowers her arms. He falls on his knees, 'gathers' the flower, protects it, 'cries' and he offers it to her again. She re-enters the game, she smells it and she puts it in her hair, she proudly turns her back to him, and leaves. Without his permission. He utters a cry of admiration*)

He (*director*): Excellent! The right move. And the right poise. You exhude exactly what you are feeling: understanding, the tact towards the individual who insists to court you, but also indifference! Because you 'have another', who is much better, more suitable for you... You were wonderful!

She: Rubbish.

He: Word of honour! I was playing and you! - You created the emotion. Oh Lord, I haven't expected it that just here, tonight, a woman... A good and sensitive woman... Please do not interrupt me. I have never believed that *precisely I* could see with my own eyes how someone who is not 'in the theatre' can communicate such feelings through a simple... Please let us resume! I... was here.

She: Stop it.

He: You, over there. Come!

She: Be serious!

He: The scene was superb! Throw the flower. But not ostentatiously, - do it for me! I wish to see it. OK?

She: You are mad...

He: I am! So, tired of my insistence, you let your arms fall down. The elbows, close to your hips, yesss... The hands slightly away from your thighs.

She (*carries it out*)

He: Good! You hold the flower and you smell it. Camera... action!

(*He resumes his position. They rehearse the scene together - which must be perfect! When they finish it, she turns towards him and waits*)

He: Thank you. Really... have you never played before?

She: In the high school.

He: You should know that you are made for the theatre.

She: Sometimes, such a thought had occurred to me, but... I chased it away. No, it was too much for me, much too much. First of all, I couldn't bear the happiness of being admitted to University...

He: I am overjoyed with enthusiasm when I meet individuals who declare themselves a knock out, without even setting one foot in the ring. You are 'a champion', my dear girl, this is written on your forehead, don't be afraid to enter the ring!... What else do you know?

She: What should I know?

He: To do! Do not irritate me. I am not overwhelmed by your performances as The Great Manual Manipulator of the Dust Cloth! I am interested in the others! (*Pause*) Come, come, come, what are you waiting for? Act on! Let yourself go, I wish to see it! At the entrance examination at drama school, you are given three words and you are asked to improvise! You have the genius, I tell you, on my happiness, what are you waiting for, Madam, to make me mad?...

She: I have not thought of...!

He: What... to think here? I let you start here on the wooden boards! Let's see it all! Tell me everything that could be said about what is bothering you: about what is burning you...! About what is making you mad here, in this institution!

She: Nothing.

He: Then what does it amuse you?

She: Everything.

He: My Lord, I have met a wise person.

She: You should know that, as the case may be, I could mock at you so that you might regret the moment you met me!

He: I wish to convince myself about you: Have you played all your cards on Saturday the 13th, or is it something else? Now *I* have come into the equation. From the night.

Sent by Providence: choose! Perhaps it is our last encounter. *Yours with yourself, through me!*

She: You must recognise you are slightly megalomaniac.

He: At last, have some courage and listen to me: I am *Somebody*, passing via *Here*, on the way to *Somewhere*. In this sentence, neither *Somebody*, nor *Here* or *Somewhere* counts. Only the sensation of flow counts; the breeze, *the passing*! 'I am Somebody... *passing* via *Here*... on the way to Somewhere...!' It is You in *Here*. You were waiting this *passing* with your *inner soul*. The passing through *Here* is touching you. Do not miss the opportunity! On my knees, I beseech you not to repeat the mistake I made once!... Perhaps I was the chosen one...! (*He takes his head into his hands. He almost shouts*) Why do I interfere? Why do I trouble your life with my suppositions? Do not listen to me! I am the bearer of bad omen, the bad omen is called *dream*! It is a deformity, a kind of humpback, it cannot be seen: you see it only after you have listened to me! But when you see it, it is too late: you have become infected; and you can only curse me. Be on your guard: you are content.

She: What do I have to do?

He: Be on your guard!

She (*irritated*): You have rattled me; tell me what I must do. Now, *I wish to see*!

He: I have told you to be on your guard! The dream is a drug: when you come here from within, you feel the need to return, because *the dream* is *the future*! It is the most dangerous vice. Some still don't know that the dream is like a plastic bomb stuck to the present moment. This will explode later! In history! Happy woman, the anti-dream vaccine must be urgently manufactured...! You must be on your guard!

She: Prove it to me that you are not a liar!

He (*sardonically*): Yes? Well...! What are you feeling now?

She: That I could strangle you!

He (*laughs*): Splendid! You are furious, aren't you? You are undecided: you don't know what to do. You don't know if to hit me on the head or cry. You feel like crying a little, don't you? It's obvious that you cry quite often. Very clear! (*He shouts.*) Tell me: am I right?

She: You are!

He (*shouts*): of course I am right!

She (*throws an object which He catches. Up*): Damn you, miserable convict! Damn you…!

He: Stay still like this! (*Calm*) Now, you start telling. Something funny. Prove to yourself that you are able! Something funny, now, when you feel like screaming! Tell it; do not act as a blockhead!

She (*unsure*): Damn you…!

He: This profession is great! Artists who had received news of bereavement proved it while performing on the stage! And they went on acting. If you have strength in you, show it! Go on! Go on!

She (*forcing a feeling of well-being*): Anything?

He: Anything!

She (*stretching*): Anyway?

He: Anyway! The play… everything is play, the play counts!

(*They play very seriously, very touching*)

She: You do not look so ugly yourself.

He: I am turning wonderful little by little! (*He makes wry faces*)

She: You are even becoming pleasant!

He (*with wry faces*): I am like an apple: I become better and sweeter as time goes by…!

She: You are good and handsome! You are straight in body, agile in mind; I haven't seen a man like you!

He (*becomes monstrous physically*): I have all the qualities envied in a man, that's why no woman has reached me…!

She: It is difficult to reach up to you, wonder of the world! The eyes see you, the ears hear you, I feel your manly smells, - poor hands, they do not reach you…! Only inanimate objects (*she takes hold of the broom.*) They caress your body!...

He (*bleats*): You are the only one who has managed to break the obstacle of my sweet feelings. They are invading my world now, they are making it according to my image!...

She: My duty is to put your feelings in one basket. Too much sweetness in this poor world!

(*She suddenly hits him with the broom*)

He (*bewildered*): What are you doing?

She (*hitting him rather hard*): Play! Do not stop! Continue! 'The play… all is a play, the play counts!' What does a certain blow mean, compared to the joy of suffering it? What does a bump represent compared to the satisfaction of 'communicating' the intense bewilderment, which overwhelms you?

(*She hits him hard. He finds refuge, croaking, behind the furniture. She chases him while hitting the objects etc. - Scene from a comic opera. She finds it funny, and she bursts into laughter. She sits on the settee*)

He (*he prudently exits from behind the armchair*): Ready?

She (*laughs*): I have cooled down.

(Silence. He stares at her and then becoming serious, he walks towards his rucksack and after searching attentively, he takes out a piece of paper)

He: Read this.

She: Your certificate of good behaviour.

He: Read loud, please.

She: I know the three r's, word of honour!

He: I would be very glad if you were to do what I am asking of you.

She: You have become so solemn!?...

He: Do not delay.

She *(looks at the paper)*: Oh, I understand!... But...! It is very beautiful... And sad. *(She reads it to herself.)* I like it *(after she finishes reading)* 'It was a river...'

He: A moment *(he closes the curtain)*

She *(from behind the curtain)*: What are you doing?!...

He *(from the front of the curtain)*: The show! The show is a ritual. Let me know when you are ready. Shall I open it?

She *(from behind the curtain)*: Not yet... The show only is a ritual, isn't it? This is what you said. I must get ready!... At the third gong, all right?

(The gong can be heard)

He: I have been waiting for you with emotion!

She: Is there a big audience?

He: The performance hall is full! When the curtain rises, the applause will convince you that you are expected.

She: Wonderful!... (The gong seems to carry on her emotion)

He: This evening is Your celebration, - you will give the last bit of Yourself. There isn't a greater joy than having the knowledge that you do not belong to yourself, is there?... We celebrate You, and let you enchant us. We celebrate

94

You, and let you cry for us. This way, we become cleaner. How good we are. We, the audience!...

She: I thank you, but you are wrong.

He: I am not wrong: you are in full celebration, Madam!

(The gong answers only: short and powerful. It is confusing. After a while, spiteful to himself, he opens the curtain to see what is happening to Her. She appears within the framed space of the curtain with a new identity: the warm image of genuine womanhood - long dress, hair falling onto her shoulders, bare feet. She raises her forehead, she recites. He sits down, he watches her)

She: 'there was a river with green banks
and a mill.
and, as any river,
it had a whirlpool

drinking its water, a doe
was to die by the fangs of a wolf
controlled by the reigns of hunger.
the children of the village
avoided it for a while
though the fish only knew of it -
they needn't have worried
for the death of the doe
was their shield

enormous silence
where she drowned
while she was playing

there lived a short girl
with blond hair

and faint smell
of basil
sorrow
and fish
called her
inner soul in solitude

was the bank too green?
had the whirlpool got power?

she lost what beings still had
and the grove suddenly
resurrected.

the beasts came to light
along flowers and grasses
in circles, butterflies
perpetuated their movement into infinity.

prudent
fish
told with their tails
what could happen if
something alike might occur

looking at the new fairy
they sensed
that the miller
was to drain the river soon.'

(He applauds frantically. On a tape, cascades of applause. She looks at the audience: so that's called success! He finds a bunch of flowers, which he offers her)

He: Congratulations! (*They greet the audience together*)

She (*whispers*): What are you doing?

He: I thank them because they are civilised.

She (*whispers*): Leave immediately... (*Bows, in the rhythm of the recorded applause*) immediately...!

He: I say... They understand that they are applauding only for you! I am grateful that they understand you. That they admire you and that they love you! (*Bow*) Look how they are applauding you... Because they love you...! Listen! (*Applause*) Have you seen this? They wish to see more of you! (*To the audience*) I thank you from the bottom of my heart! I embrace you all! You are the most wonderful audience I have ever met!... Thank you. In a way to understand means to create! You have created... *this*! (*He points towards Her with a large gesture*) Applaud her!... Once again! (*Loud applause on the tape*) Applaud her at home, go and tell about her! Applaud her at work, in your thoughts. Remember to applaud her when you are alone! Because, on these boards, she is *alone* and she gives herself to each one of you!

She (*bows*): If you do not leave I shall burst into tears! Please!... All the town will say that you are mad and they will say about me that...

He: In front of everybody... (*To the audience*) Silence, please! In front of everybody, I declare that you are wonderful!

She: Why are you doing this?

He: I declare you are the greatest actress I know!

She: I liked the verse, that's why! They are so strange...

He: I almost envy you.

She: Let's not exaggerate after all.

He: I invite you to... a restaurant!

She: My break came when I met someone who could adore me! Be serious. (*She laughs*)

He: I go to change my clothes. I shall put on the white blazer and the violet trousers. And you?

She: I?

He: You can go in this dress...

She: I cannot go in this dress...

He: Then? What are you going to wear?

She: I would like something else. I would like...

He: A fur!

She (*laughs*): A fur, in August?

He: Then, a Safari suit!

She: I wish... (*She points to the audience*) I wonder if they might like, if... (*To the audience*) I would like to wrap up in rolls of heavy Chinese taffeta. A deep décolleté in 'V', I shall match it with elongated pink and white pearls, and on my hips, as a suggestion to a lawn extension, a vegetal landscape, as if it were climbing. I shall wear long fingerless gloves decorated with pearls and false diamonds; a boa of African ostrich feathers on my shoulders; thin long tights of fine silk, with a vague line of silver Lycra, but the shoes... My pointed stiletto shoes, reminding, when I walk, of the mad rhythm of Charleston!... Men, I am sure that if you were to see me often, you'd love and respect me more...! Am I... right? (*She bursts into tears.*) Will you respect me... even more?... You'll tell yourselves that I also need some understanding, a little love, the banal question: 'hey, you, how are you?'

He (*scared of how things are turning*): Talk to me! There aren't any people there! The performance hall is empty!

She: It is not true! Do not lie to me! These chairs are full! (*To the audience*) I shall ask you a question, only one: are you unable to love me because I am who I am? Can't you respect me?... Can't we be friends? Really, it isn't compulsory to be very beautiful; if, in my imagination only, I were to abandon my children for you?...

He: Relax. You are crying like a servant girl!

She: Why am I wearing this dress?

He: We had fun!

She: Yes?

He: Of course... we had! And it was great. It was great... up to now to be precise.

She: Did we have fun?!... Did we have fun?!

He: You'll have another fit: like on the balcony, when you went to think!

She: But I told you that I swore not to attempt it again!... Why did you let me?... Lord, what foolishness!... Help me! I don't understand what is happening to me... Help me!...

He (*with unlimited sadness*): You are condemned: you have learnt that you... you are not... just a body! You have learnt that you are also... someone else. My Lady...

She: I am not *a lady*! I am a poor cleaner, a prop that does not understand what you have done to her...! Where have I gone wrong!?

He: Calm yourself: they cannot touch us. It has happened!

She: Oh Lord, the children!...

(*She is running along the performance hall towards the exit*)

He: Do not go out like this into the town!

She: Be cursed!

He: Do not go yet! For a few moments, you lived another life! I only wanted to help you...!

She: I didn't need *this*!!... I hate you!... Those who are like me, do not have the right to this, do not need this!... (*She shouts*) I have a family!... I have children, I have my own life, I am happy! I am really happy! You are only a convict who brings bad luck with you!... (*Bewildered by what she said, she holds her hands to Him. With* *bewilderment*) What has really made Maria wait for you?!...

(*She bursts into floods of tears. Immense happiness covers her face. Darkness, silence*)

THE CURTAIN

OH LORD, MAKE SCHNAUZER WIN!
(Doamne, fă ca Schnauzer să câstige!)[3]

The meaning of the names encountered in this drama:

1. **DANIIL** - The Lord is my judge;
2. **MARA** - grief;
3. **EVA** - life.

A lock up cell in the dangerous inmates' pavilion. The door with spy-hole in the wall at the back, the window above the ribalta, (through which a thread of light filters into the cell from the dirty bulb of the rubbish skip where the spectators are placed), above, a watch chamber in the corner on the left.

Somewhere, a giant screen.

The sufferings and the noise of the gaol are perceived with hysterical clarity.

---

[3] **Printed in the volumes:** *„Jocuri (de unu, de doi...)"*, P.H. Junimea, Iaşi, 1998; *„Doamne, fă ca Schnauzer să câştige!"*, P.H. Casa scriitorilor, Bacău, 2004; *„Doamne, fă ca Schnauzer să câştige!"*, (Romanian, English, German and French variants), P.H. Valman, Râmnicu Sărat, 2010 and in the culture magazine *„Baadul literar"*, (2009, 3rd year, number 4).

Performed at: Dramatic Theatre „Andrei Mureşanu", Sfântu Gheorghe, theatrical season 2000, director Adrian Ancuţa and Tiberiu Tudoran; Municipal Theatre „Bacovia", Bacău, theatrical season 2005-2006, director Adrian Găzdaru; „Pygmalion" Theatre, Viena, theatrical season 2006, (reading-shows), director Geirun Tino, translated into German by Dan Stoica.

The convict is guilty of having understood by far too early that the greatest part of his guilt is to be found in the company of the other individuals, that liberty is an invention and that the gaol is the place where you are.

Yesterday I – In the Evening

On the screen, a flux of different images, amongst which: newlyweds, - here I have found Mara and Daniil -, a fashion show, light music soloists, dancers etc., etc.

Sometimes the images were frozen by the projection of some newspaper titles like: 'The Social Bomb' – 'The Poaching of Transition'... - 'Soon Two Little Girls from Botoşani Will Die of Aids' – 'The Marriage of the Century'- 'The AGA Feast' – 'A Possible Miracle: the Discovery of the Antidote against Aids!' - 'From Cover-Girl to Star' – 'The Chechens Will Surrender Their Weapons' – 'Aids – In Brief!' – 'The Minister of Health Violates the WHO Norms' – 'And Bardot Is on Holiday'.

On the stage, Daniil, dressed in striped trousers and a vest execises.

A VOICE: Attention! (*Daniil stands to attention.*) Come in front of the lens of the camera. Come closer. (*Daniil comes closer.*) Smile! Number.

DANIIL: 4979!

A VOICE: How do you feel?

DANIIL: I am aching under the left shoulder blade: from the latest interrogation! And I have cramps.

A VOICE: Are you content with the regime of detention?

DANIIL (*answers bluntly*): I have cramps!

A VOICE: We do not understand what you want to demonstrate... Two extra days of solitary confinement have been added to your previous conviction. You will spend a total of 28 days here. For the time being!

DANIIL (*subdued*): Please, no! I beg for your forgiveness!

A VOICE: Are you content with the regime of detention?

DANIIL: I am very, very content!...

A VOICE: Excellent! You have been left with 28 days of solitary confinement. Out of which, you still have to atone for five.

DANIIL: You are far too generouswith me.

A VOICE: March into the corner! (*Daniil obeys*) To bed! (*Daniil settles on the cement*) All are content and nobody wants anything. Lights off...!

(*It has become dark*)

DANIIL (*after a while*): Again, again, again...! Nothing changes...! Nothing changes... Nothing...

II – Today – In the Evening

On the screen, the same atmosphere as 'Yesterday Evening'. Daniil is on his knees.

DANIIL: I did what I did to reach you, to make you better!... Haven't you considered that she was a child, - and you stood against us though we did not sin!?... I have always helped others and you allowed everybody to turn against me - as if you wished to teach me against your teachings that it is not good for me to act kindly to others?... My kindness was rewarded with evil; following your path successfully caused hatred and envy in those around me; being kind and helping those unfortunate labelled me as a hypocrite. Honesty drove my friends away, my correctness multiplied my enemies, and my purity excluded me from society. You did not show me any friendship when I followed your teachings and I modelled myself according to them - I

103

hope I am not wrong for searching for You outside, or perhaps You are within me? - My Lord, I blaspheme again. (*Pause*) They were asleep... the moon was out, Eva was asleep face up, Mara was protecting her; she had her arm over her tiny body - in the dim light, her face looked worried, widening the wrinkles of bitterness at the corner of her lips, Eva was smiling happily in her sleep - both of them beautiful and sensible as I would have liked them to remain forever, I would have liked them free - Mara of fears, Eva of the pain caused by children, by their parents and teachers...! - Life is a gaol...death is an exile. **I have exiled them to save them!...** Have I been gaoled for this?!... You keep the witness of your crime gaoled, because you forced me to commit it! Because Eva was ill, you got scared and you sealed the doors of the school! You sent them away with hypocritical excuses; you scared them! You took away their last chance, what kind of people are you, what do you call this? Are you human beings?

Anyway Eva would die soon. Mara would commit suicide, and I would be left alone without meaning a big deal... I killed them in order to absolve the earth of a suffering which could have been scattered into the wind, in order to make you aware that you are not alone, that it is a sin to hide behind one's duty, and that on this earth grief multiplies more than duckweed on a waveless lake, because man is a very good conductor of sorrow. (*He laughs reservedly*) Locked... The clever ones...! The earth is a gaol, the continent is a gaol, home is a gaol, and the body is a gaol from which one cannot exit. -

...The bars and the walls have two faces. Who is inside, who is outside? (*He speculates*) If those from inside agree with those from outside that they are inside, then it is certain they are inside: if the ones from outside agree with the ones from inside that they are outside, then they are certainly outside, - **as I endorse that they are**! -, and the ones outside say that it is a lie, because they are outside, then we can expect a civil war; or… a revolution; or a riot; or a coup d'état; or… a government decision… Damn this life!... Which is a gaol and death an exile. (*He shouts*) Therefore, a kind of liberty! Without you…! You hold on it with your teeth, although life uses you less and less or more and more… Neither your hate matters any more! Nor your atrocious selfishness, dragging hatred towards the death you do not deserve! (*He shouts*) I exiled them with good reason: in order to save them!... I saved them from this maddening debate with **the inside and… the outside**…

- As about my wife and my daughter suffering from Aids, both those **inside** as well as **outside** decided that they are both inside, therefore locked, condemned to solitude for ever…!

I saved then by exiling them there… where they cannot be… but outside! (*He screams*) Murderers! Murderers!... How could you not allow my good child, my Eva to start her first day at school near her peers, the children?... How had you orchestrated it that they avoided her and they chased her away like a dog, with stones and with words, which both she and they did not understand?... But they were yours: your dirty words your hypocritical words, your killing words, murderers!

I did not commit suicide afterwards for I wish to learn, I wish to save you by making you look at how much I am suffering for what you made me do!... Mur… (*The door opens. Two guards enter and start hitting him methodically*) Murderers!...

*(He is beaten up in silence; methodically and with great imagination. DANIIL reacts normally, like any man hit in the face, in the stomach, over the head, in the kidneys, but silent: **beating is part of his atonement, and his groans might diminish his pain!***

The guards beat him in silence because... swearing could distract the victim's attention from the blows, and torture could diminish its intensity.

After the guards got tired, they sort each other's uniform, they wipe each other's sweat from their forehead, and they retire satisfied.)

DANIIL *(after them)*: Oi, you still haven't told me from which side the sun rises here!... Tell me: from which side does it rise? And... what day is it today? - My Schnauzer, my pedigree dog takes part in the competition and... *(The guards leave after they stare at him)*. Damn you butchers! *(He fills in his chest with air as if ready for an enormous scream, he covers his mouth with his hand, and he exhales out with fear)* Heh! *(Afterwards, he lets off steam in whisper with no one present, and surprised he laughs)* He, he!... Skilled boys... - how well they worked on me, as if from a book!... It is, ah!... They broke one of my teeth...! Greetings, marmalade! I shall not be able to eat it: I shall have terrible ache when tasting sweet. And hot. And cold. *(He checks his teeth)* They did a good job they broke it lengthwise. It will become infected in a month or two. As it happened to Mara. She was eating a hot cheese pie, and when she burnt herself, immediately... Crack, on the spot! It cracked. *(Specifying)* The tooth! She still had a cheek like a melon after three months. Eva rocked her head, pressed it between her arms smelling of sweet pie and honey,

106

and she consoled her lovingly. 'Don't worry mama, we'll beat them! Do not cry, we'll bet them' – 'Who, my darling?' – 'The tooth!...'

Eva was great... I believe she had genius.

One day, after a warm rain, I found her crying on the shores of the Bahlui River. I got scared: she was not speaking and she was pointing with her stretched arms at a boat made out of a newspaper, which was overturned amongst the branches. The boat was taking water and was sinking fast. Immense tears were flowing down her cheeks; she was silent and she was desperately staring at the little boat, which was slowly turning into a paper ball. 'What has happened, Eva?' – 'It has drowned!... I wanted to leave with mama by boat...!' – 'Where?' – 'Far away.' – 'Why, my little girl?!' – 'Because our teeth ache here...!'

Her milk teeth were rotted by sweets and she was receiving treatment at a private dental practice; the dentist didn't know... of the disease with which one of them had infected her. When we left the dental cabinet, we would take the dental drill home, and all the used dental instruments... - I did not wrong anyone, I always looked after my peers, I did not hate them because an idiotic assistant had made my child ill... Anyway, she didn't like it here any more: 'You wanted to leave me alone?' – 'I wanted to leave with mama because our teeth ache here...!'

(*He holds his head in his hands and he cries. Voices in the corridor*)

I - Oi, you, let's have a bit of fun...! Shall we try?

II - No point: we've just beaten him; I don't think he is in high spirits.

I - What high spirits? Which high spirits? I am telling you the wretch is suffering from ţupa-ţupa! Let's start the music and... ready, he will start at once!

II - Do you believe he is so stupid?

I - He is mad! He will not even last four minutes and he will start to jump. Let's bet!

II - But I say he lasts!

I - He will fill his pants up in three minutes! Bet on five dollars!

II - Then, make him step on the gas. Let's see!

I - Five dollars?

II - Done.

DANIIL (*hopeful*): Hey! Hey!... Can you tell me, what day is it today?

I - Open the peephole!

II - But are you sure that the commandant has gone home?

DANIIL: My dog Schnauzer takes part in the competition, I must know, he is the only member of my family left outside: my only friend, you have no right...!

I - Open the peephole, mister, damn you, do it! Are you dragging it?

II - If the commandant hasn't gone home?

I - But, do you want to win five dollars? Yes or no?

(The peephole opens. A loud speaker can be heard from outside)

II - Switch on the music!

(The ravishing rhythm of a devilish dance can be heard)

DANIIL: If you please, not this time! If you do not tell me what day it is today, no!... Idiots, do you enjoy the suffering of a handicapped man? Does a man's condition amuse you? What day is it today? *(He tries not to dance).* What's the date today? Is it Saturday, is it Sunday? Is it Monday? *(The music amplifies, the rhythm becomes more alert, and DANIIL tries to control himself with all his might and not to let himself at the will of his irrepressible dancing urges)* Surely, it's April, but what date is it? The competition is On Sunday, the 4th, but when?: today or tomorrow?

(He is captivated by the rhythm, against his urging will)

DANIIL: Is today tomorrow, yesterday or today? *(He covers the music)* I want to know what day it is today! I wish to celebrate my friend the dog, my Schnauzer, for his victory at the international dog competition! I wish to know what day it is today! I wish to know what's the date today! If today is tomorrow, yesterday was the day before yesterday, then, when is it the 4th of April? Has it already been? Was it yesterday, will it be the day after tomorrow?... *(He dances tremendously with the objects, with his own clothes - devastatingly).* What does it matter?... I dance because it is good for me. I like it a lot!... Do you think that I am also mad!... A little, a little mad...

(He dances on his knees. The music stops abruptly. One can hear and see how the speaker is removed from the peephole. DANIIL melts to the floor)

II - Ha, ha, you have lost...! Put down the money!

I - You arranged it with the scoundrel beforehand. He didn't feel like dancing, like that, unexpectedly, after the beating he got!

II - Five in all! Five, we agreed: money down, jackanapes!

I - Damn you…, let's go to the changing room!

(He slams the peephole noisily. DANIIL breathes heavily. He collapses completely, he would like that every one of his cells sticks to the floor. After a while, rubbing his chin and his nose against the cement, he looks up. He stares at the audience fearfully, as if he were in the trenches. He utters something, which cannot be heard, with an expression of imploration and terror on his face. - Something distracts his attention: It is a cockroach. He is fighting between the desire to stare at the audience and the desire to take care of the cockroach. He masters his second impulse. He laughs menacingly)

DANIIL: Mister… cockroach. You are back again… No, no, no, no! Remain here, if you haven't respected my order… *(He stealthily hurries like a cat, to place the hollow of his palm over it)* Damn you; stay still, when I am telling you! *(He lifts his palm slightly)*. I warned you last time that, if I caught you within my territory again, I should kill you. *(With fierce satisfaction)* Now, I shall kill you! *(He lifts his palm, he gets ready to crash it, stop! his grin disappears, a thoughtful and stern expression sets on his face)* But if you are not the one which I summoned? Because you resemble amazingly to one another… I cannot do you an injustice. Are you many? Do you live inside the rubbish bin, *(He looks at the audience)*, you rake the world's garbage, you multiply, you eat, you climb, and rob one another, but you greet each other with respect,

110

(*He waves his arms up to his temples, like the antennae of an insect - or like a human greeting?*), you always dress in a shining suit, to show you are somebody, but you are still living out of rubbish and you feel good in rubbish too!... We might have never met, as you are not aware of the rules established by me here, therefore, it is possible that you are innocent. However... however... however... how on earth do I know that you are not changing places amongst yourselves in order to annoy me?

Look what I have found: I shall mark you with toothpaste! And if you march here, without my permission, I shall flatten you! (*He puts a straw into the toothpaste tube and he places a mark on its back*) Now, go away! (*He places the tube in his pocket*) Aren't you going? Very good. Do you want an explanation - you must also tell the others where you are coming from, my point of view: to kill someone from another species is a right, which, personally, I consider criminal - but I obey, if everybody does the same. - You haven't understood. Somebody, a supreme being: the Lord or some superior and intelligent entity that we do not understand creates various species following the fundamental laws of symmetry and according to a unique system of organization of the organic matter, when it had time on its hands: insects, reptiles, mammals etc., even plants. And, in its wisdom, it has decided that all, even if they might be relatives through conception, should survive destroying one another.

Have you understood? I am not eating you because, these gaolers here give me enough to survive for the time being.

Have you put this in your head? And now, shoo home! (*He pushes it with the straw*)

111

Tell your lot that I am a fair big bug - with fewer legs but with greater soul; I have eaten my fill but my mind is hungry; poor in this world and poor… but rich in my heart; accused by those gaolers of being guilty, guilty only because I am demanding my right to give up. (*He is looking up to the window*). What are You saying, Old Man? What have You turned us into?... What is the use of it?... You can be proud that we do not understand You. We follow You so little…! Perhaps that's why. - When You created the beings… You made them lacking imagination…! The snake, the dog, the pig and the frog; the cow, the whale, the monkey and the lion; the duck, the camel, the seal and the man - all, what a desperate monotony! They were all made to be an equal Second. You, being… First! Second means the regress of the First, because all strive to be First: two hemispheres of the brain, two eyes, two ears, two lungs, two nostrils, two canines, and two pairs of limbs.

Each group from the Second category scores a smaller First than Yours: the brain, a thought seldom like mine, the eyes, a scowling look, the ears, a hare's hearing, the lungs, breathing refrained by fear, the canines, an unjust punishment, the limbs, a chase! What have You achieved by making so many caricatures of Yourself! You were afraid, that's why You gave us so many shortcomings? Are You so sorry for having created us that You urge us to kill one another, without any compassion? - We are made in Your image and in Your likeness, Old Man, You are saying it and I like to believe You, but man is the most disgusting being I know: greedy against his fellow creature, selfish, treacherous, hypocritical; the coward who invented what You haven't even thought of: the Truth-Lie and the Lie-Truth - alas, how much You have been surpassed in cynicism, Old Man!... Do not be proud of tMan any more: through his own being, Man is against the beauty of Your creation. (*Tired*) Old Man, Your perfection is made of secretions only; Man digests, expectorates, urinates, sweats, defecates, salivates, has dandruff, has wax in his ears, and has tears in his eyes and above all, he stinks! Old Man, You made a mess of it, in this respect, You rushed things. You were also tired... You had made so many other things before You created us... Old Man, You only one perfect accomplishment, in which You are entirely complete with everything that is good in You: the childhood. **The childhood of all beings!** The puppy wolf plays with the puppy dog, together they play with the human baby and they sleep together with the baby bear hugging the tiger cub without any care in the world.

Oh, Lord! Old Man! One cries tears of joy when one can see them push one another so that they can enjoy tumbling with each other!...

Without any purpose and only out of enjoyment, - why will You let them grow up if they become bad enemies?...

Eva was one of the most formidable children whom I met in my joyless life. She had answers to everything, she was thinking of the world and its forces; I always held my breath when she was answering to a question about something unknown.

She was three years old. We were celebrating Maria's birthday and we were walking along the alley of springs at Slănic Moldova Spa; the three of us were holding each other's hand.

I stopped at spring no.15 to drink the water prescribed for after-a-drinking-spree. Mara also joined us. 'Will you drink it, Eva?' - 'I don't drink it' – 'Why?'- 'I don't like it' – 'It is spring water, my darling!' – 'I don't like it!'... 'Do you know what a spring is?' She

113

answered in a huff: 'Yes!' – 'What is a spring?' - Still sulking: 'There where the mountain does a wee!'…Ha, ha, ha! How much Mara could laugh…! I was looking at her speechless; that very moment, I knew it precisely that I had a gifted child. And I cried. Mara was laughing and I was crying. I was crying with joy: perhaps Eva might have represented something in our imperfect world. (*Crying*) Eva!... My wonderful little girl!... My good child: the only reason for which I must suffer You so that I can protect Mara from You. Eva felt that what she was discovering around her was alive and it had a soul with which - probably in her purity - she could communicate. A peeled off house upset her because it had 'a bruise'. The leaves of an almost dead tree were rustling because it was… 'old and it was holding to the sky in order not to fall down'. The stream 'was laughing', the forest 'was speaking nonsense', and the mountain 'was asleep because it was tired…' – 'Daddy, isn't the forest too heavy for the mountain?' – 'No, my little girl!' - I heard her: 'rubbish' - 'That's how it is!' – 'It's silly and heavy, why doesn't the mountain throw it down…?'

Do You hear it, Old Man? Why doesn't the mountain stand up and shake the forest off? - What about that? Well? Perhaps You could finish us faster, and You could also save Yourself from us, of the trouble we might cause… - Mara wasn't at all impressed: 'Nonsense, Dani!... Nonsense Dani… Nonsense…'

How much she loved me! (*Shouting*) Nobody has loved me as much as Mara! They couldn't have loved me, because nobody, except her, could have understood me! Yes!

Even now, from where she is now, near You Lord, she is looking at me, she understands me and she forgives me for what I did to her; to her and to her little girl; because (*He screams*) she knew that it couldn't have been any different!... She knows it and she has forgiven me, wretched criminals who pushed me to kill her... (*He wheezes*) My little girl didn't live long and Mara would have committed suicide anyway...

The few days left to me to deceive myself had been embittered by our isolation... Why were You so heartless not to allow her to be with her peers?... It was the only human celebration in which she could have taken part - and you interdicted her! Out of hysteric fear. - I did not have the right... I had to save them! They were far too good, and they were like two saints! I should have saved them.

I know that Mara agrees, Mara loved me and she knows that I did it out of love...- Outside... there, I had no one, except our Schnauzer dog, named Schnauzer, which is the best. (*He gets into a state of anxiety; he paces up and down, from here to there*) The competition takes place, or has taken place, or it will take place... on the 4th of April. I have no news or visits here - locked up, but Hary takes care, he is a very correct Jew. (*He suddenly laughs*) He, what hasn't he done for his brother!...- 'Oi Oscar, you do only foolish things... Oi, you behave so foolishly that you make me, your good brother, become anti-Semitic...!' - Oh Lord, what has crossed his mind!... But, if Hary has become your friend, he is your friend until death!...- 'Oh Lord, DANIIL, listen to me: I am a Jew, but these Romanians who did not allow your child in school, are a stinking lot!..' - (*Pause*)

He takes care, he will show them, what our Schnauzer can do, my darling Mara! Devoted, intelligent, vigorous and robust Schnauzer will humiliate them: it will be successful in a way they are not and will never be! With certainty...!

115

'Yes, Mr Hary, I wish that Schnauzer revenges us. I wish that it would have the public success, which my little girl, my wife and I never enjoyed! I wish for Schnauzer to win! It is very important to us, Mr Hary...!'(*In tears*) We did not even have the joy of a little crown: Eva, our clever little girl, was not allowed to compete with any one...! (*Resolute*) Schnauzer is intelligent! Yes! It has a strong elongated head, wet and oval shaped dark coloured eyes, pointed ears - always straight and a well built body, a nervous short body, with muscular shoulders. Silver-grey, with wiry rough hair... It has bushy eyebrows - they cover his eyes, which are full of love and trust... It will win! It will win, Mr Hary! If it were not to win, that means that some mean trick might have occurred. (*Pause*) Damn wretch, what's the date today?

Oh Lord, how can I find out?

I could swallow an object so they could take me to the infirmary, I could drink poison or something strong, but they have made sure in advance that there is no possibility for me to escape from here. The walls are smooth, there is no chair, and no table but the potty... what can I do with a potty? If I shout, they come and they hit me again. (*He grins*) They like to do it a lot!... They believe that I am an important force descended from the high spheres and, because they will never get there, they take revenge against me and they beat me. Healthy! It is a kind of therapy: afterwards, they feel content and a bit comforted: someone from their world of dirty warders will not be in for something like this!... - This, only if they are not vicious and they do it for their own pure pleasure, which is not impossible. They are also people, it is important to feel strong, it is important to like the work one is paid for, it is very important to feel secure; it is vital that there is one weaker than you at least.

Corrupt, merciless, perverse and hypocrite! (*Pause*)

Even the Commandant himself suggested organizing an escape for me!?... To reach Milan, where my case would be publicised all over the Globe! My photograph, Mara and Eva's would end up in all the newspapers of the world, on all the TV screens, in front of all the families... And, with my story, I would help the collection of funds for the fight against the HIV and I wouldn't be extradited!

All the campaign would be called Eva that is LIFE - the name of my child...

They have not understood anything...!

You have not understood anything!

I did what I had done in order to save them. I did what I had done in order to help them. I did what I had done so that you understand how evil you are, that, fundamentally, you are only some diseased ferocious beasts with little, very little reason placed in the service of your instinct of survival. The so-called human behaviour is generated by cowardice, lies and hypocrisy, - serious vices which automatically exclude any carnivorous creature from the community. These vices unite you and make you accomplices... My backside is more sincere than your faces, which do not tire to mimic sincerity!

Oh Lord, I should not speak like this, but what can I do? Anyway, I exclude any co-operation: **I must atone for it! I shall be useful only in this manner.** Thus I shall make them pay attention to me and I... I shall truly become useful... (*Up*) My spirit kills the older brother born before: the body. And it kills it little by little through torture - didactic and purifying fratricide...- are you worth it? (*He sits cross-legged on*

the floor, he arduously sings a Priceasnă after which)
You abandoned your little body, Eva... - We got
accustomed to talk about our bodies when we refer to
one another, though we, the true ones are inside these
organisms, which carry us... - You feel better now. -
Why can't you reveal yourself without your body of
milk and biscuits?... (*Pause*) Because I am a man...!
Perhaps because you were just a body...

- 'Daniil! Eva sprained her leg!'...- 'Mara, Eva
burned her little finger!' – 'Schnauzer, to your place!
You have thrown Eva down' – 'Oi, get up, you are
dropping the baby!' - I was on the bus, I hadn't slept
for two days and I was taking her to Hary. Mara and I
had been brought up in an orphanage... That's why we
loved each other so much: we had only each other. We
did not sleep for three days, both of us lived by
drinking coffees, Eva was the only one who was eating.
We would go out at night - we couldn't bear to see our
neighbours avoid us because the whole district had
learnt of Eva's infection because of the incident at
school. One might have shouted: 'Why don't you go to
France, Mister, because otherwise you will infect
everyone of us.' The knave of the mayor had found the
solution: 'But it is not compulsory for your little girl to
start school when she is six! Wait another year. Until
then... - he was embarrassed - she'll grow up! That is
she'll be older...' - That is she may die! 'And we have
mountains, the little girl is... delicate, she needs fresh
air. I understand that it is easier for you to keep her
near you but you should make a small sacrifice for the
child: how much would it cost you? Take her to
relatives!'

Eva and Mara wanted toast with butter and honey.
How much they played school, I prepared a thick syrup

from an infusion of lime blossom, which was very much like honey.

Mara asked me for a Phenobarbital or Diazepam tablet so that she could fall asleep: she was finished off from crying and the vigil. The idea came to me. It couldn't go any longer: I had to decide somehow. And I decided!

Did you see how well I acted? Did you see how you were overcome by compassion? Did you see how many mourners were present and accompanied them on their last journey, after they had been persecuted and insulted day in and day out? (*Proud*) Iaşi had never seen such a funeral! Thousands of people cried together in the streets of Iaşi. For my darling girls: my wife, my only relative in this world and my daughter, Eva, my little Jesus, sacrificed so that we could become better people. Think of Eva: innocent, credulous, crying for you had condemned her because of fear - you could have been in her place, and Eva would not have condemned you, she would have rocked you in her little arms and she would have calmed you as only angels know how.

Had you protected Eva, or had you accepted her at least, you could have had a chance. But now... I am the only one left; I shall try to cure you...

What I am most afraid of is that I resemble you. It will be a tragedy. It would mean that my sacrifice was made out of interest. Oh, Lord, this is not possible; I couldn't play such a dirty trick on Mara!

(*He shouts*) I do not resemble you; I am ashamed to resemble you! I feel sick, I am disgusted, I am different!... (*Tired, he breathes heavily*) I am different. I must be different; otherwise it does not make any sense! - Mara was telling me... (*He laughs*) Ha, ha, ha! Mara was telling me that I was like apricot in milk. - I used to mix crushed seeds with cubes of scented apricots, and sprinkle all with a little sugar.

It can be a special treat! But... ha, ha, ha!... the cramps begin after twelve minutes, on the clock. Which are like some reptile twists in one's stomach. 'He, he, I was laughing, apricots in milk may spoil one's stomach, but in the loo... they leave an unequal exotic smell, something between a brioche and... putrid cockroaches! Don't they? It is something!' - She would watch me disgusted and she would tell me I was silly but she really paid me a compliment; too many good things for one man, which he didn't really deserve because all was in vain... a bit of venom and malice were needed - a little, a little interest there, only from You, would have been good, like salt in food...!

I did not understand her. My kindness and hers are like... a bit of faeces from the apricot in milk mixture...!

...Because someone dared to stroke her hair in my presence, I made a collar for him out of the table!

I took her by the hand and I left. Mara was roaring with laughter, - 'You silly Billy, you silly Billy...!' - , that person's friends were trying to remove the table out of his neck; the plywood became fissured when it was moved over his ears and it caught him like in a vice: the ram was screaming... Ha, ha, ha! 'Damn stupid, damn stupid...'

A VOICE: Attention! (*DANIIL stands to attention*) Come in front of the camera. Come closer. (*DANIIL gets closer*) Smile!... Number!

DANIIL: 4979!

A VOICE: How are you feeling?

DANIIL: Could you please tell me what's the date today...

A VOICE: Are you content with the detention regime?

DANIIL (*impatient*): I asked you to tell me what's the date today; don't I have the right to know it?

A VOICE: We don't understand what you want to demonstrate?!... Three extra days in solitary confinement are added to your sentence. You'll spend a total of 31 days here. For now!

DANIIL (*scared*): If you please, no! Please forgive me, if you please!

A VOICE: Are you content with the detention regime?

DANIIL (*in a hurry*): I am very content, more than content!...

A VOICE: Excellent. You have only 31 days of solitary confinement. You still have seven left to do.

DANIIL: Thank you, please forgive me for...!

A VOICE: March to the corner. (*DANIIL obeys*) Lights off! (*DANIIL lies on the floor*) Everybody is content, and nobody wants anything. It is... Lights off!

(*Total darkness*)

DANIIL: (*after a while, in the dark*): Again, again, again... Nothing changes... nothing changes... Nothing...

(*Silence. The sounds of the gaol. From the ceiling, bits of polystyrene, papers and cloths are thrown into the rubbish skip placed where the audience sits. The rustle of the insects in the papers, the comings and goings and the squeaking of the rats, the desperate meow of a cat, the aching yelp of a dog, the terrified scream of a man. Silence. A soothing melody on the panpipes suddenly stops. Light*)

III – Tomorrow – In the Evening

On the screen, photographs from the DANIIL's family album. Images for some extra action: newspaper titles and fragments of news about AIDS.
Daniil will be placed in front of the peephole with the spoon, mug and bowl in his hand. A small service hatch will open in the lower half of the door.

A VOICE: Hand over the bowl!

(Daniil will quickly bend and he will place the bowl on the floor, after which he will stand to attention)

A VOICE: Hand over the mug!

(Daniil will place the mug on the floor. In the hurry, he will drop the spoon and in a desperate attempt to catch it, he will throw it in the middle of the room. He will run after it, he will return near the peephole and he will stand to attention)

A VOICE: Is it clumsiness or is it a protest?

(Daniil will emphasize his standing to attention position looking ahead more concentrated, his chest out)

A VOICE: Do you refuse to answer?

DANIIL: I do not know what to answer to make it all right, bless you!

A VOICE (*after a while*): Bravo, you begin to understand the regime: your solitary confinement is reduced by one hour.
DANIIL: Thank you, bless you!

A VOICE: Hand over the spoon!

DANIIL: (*the same movement, the same position*)

A VOICE: At ease!

DANIIL: (*he will remain standing for a long time*)

A VOICE (*will laugh with satisfaction*): Ha, ha, ha, excellent!... A further four hours are reduced from your sentence. (Harshly) At ease, go!

DANIIL (*will execute. With his back to the camera, he will make a vulgar gesture with satisfaction*) Where in hell do you wish to take me with your system of training? If I become a submissive character, a submissive imbecile, will you kiss my backside?... (*He laughs*) If you guarantee it, I shall become one! A good citizen is only one to whom the state managed to perfectly administer a cerebral enema. In my case... the state hit against the wall; I am part of those who ask questions - those who have, what horror!... and are expecting news... Why am I expecting them, when I know that no news means good news? Having said that... here, I am overwhelmed... by wonderful news!... What stupidity: 'one experiences true happiness only in complete solitude!'. This philosophy isn't good here. It does not agree with the climate! (*He will huddle in a corner*)... I took away more than their lives, I took their future away!... Because, where you can see beauty I saw ugliness. That's why there is no fairplay in what I did and in what I am doing now: it is a journey! And whatever might happen to my body, what I do here is also called a journey: a journey into my innerself, trying to urge you to travel into your own innerselves, too. - The escape from oneself through a stupid trial. You might be forced to return so that you do not die as a beast...

Travelling outside, (*He will recite*) 'One extracts from the journey bitter wisdom/ **Yesterday**, the world was small, monotonous and ordinary,/ **Today** and **tomorrow**, our live mirror will point to:/ A sad oasis in a desert full of trouble…'

- A sad, dusty… and selfish oasis!... They had been the only really beautiful human beings who I have ever met! Above all beings and above all things and... Above all thoughts: beautiful, exceedingly beautiful!...

After they had fallen asleep, after they had begun their eternal sleep, - Eva was face up and Mara was protecting her little body with her freckled naked arm -, I kissed them. But they were not feeling me: they had escaped forever.

I stuck a note on the wardrobe: **'I tried to save them from you!'** I took a loaf of bread in my hand, - I woke up on a train, at two hundred km from Iaşi, pressing the bread to my chest and crying, I got off and I made a call. Two days and two nights I walked along the railway line - the bread got filthy; I gave myself up **when I was sure that the whole world** learnt from newspapers what had happened and **everybody knew that hate cannot always impress the world and that only love can make it go forward!**

(Steps can be heard that stop outside the door. He shudders; he anxiously jums onto his feet)

DANIIL: Oi! Stop for a moment! I have the right to know what's the date today! (He will scream) If not…!

(The door will open and another detainee will be pushed in. This detainee will not utter a word but he will display a terrible fear towards DANIIL. All the time, he will huddle against the door he entered)

124

DANIIL (*to the newcomer*): What's the date today?... What day is it today?... Call me DANIIL; do you know what day is it today? Which one? Do you understand me?... - It cannot be possible..., but I haven't forgotten to speak like a man... (*Accomplice*) They tried to confuse you; they drummed lies into your head. Sometimes they do the same to me: They lengthen my day. When my eyes are closed, they shout in the loud speaker that it is noon - time only! I must stay awake; it is very unpleasant. Some other time, they call lights out with each watch. Damn it, who can sleep then?!... And then, again, another long day... I have lost count. At the beginning I kept count of the days with bits of bread there near the wall. But the bugs came from the rubbish bins and they stole them; they carried them to their places, fsh, fshshsh!... (*He will laugh*) Ha, ha, ha! I mean that they stole my days. Doesn't this amuse you? (*Bewildered*) Now... Be sure not to...!? Try to lay down the stakes. I implore you! Do you wish to imply that you don't understand what I am saying!... It is true I have not spoken to a man for ages - I speak to the spy camera when I wake up and when I go to sleep, but anyway... it would be madness!... (*He will hold his head in his hands*) Does that mean that the guards, who beat me, don't answer me because they do not understand me? Or... because they do not hear me? - (*And even more frightened*) that is to say that what I hear are my thoughts only - and that I haven't got a voice any more?!... (*Resolute*) Speak please! (*He will scream*) Speak so I can learn if I can still hear a man's words! You, speak! So that I can learn if I can speak only... to loud speakers...! (*The new inmate will press himself even more against the door through which he entered and he will look at DANIIL with real fear*) ...Oi, you are scared of me!... Look, I am moving away from you. Calm down. Try to use your brain. We are in the same mess together: there is no reason for me to put a chain round your neck. And you shouldn't try either... Calm down, for God's sake man, why are you so terrified? (*He will point to him with his finger.*) Look at this finger. Like this. Follow it. (*He will move it*) Good. Say: 'This finger is my cell colleague's finger' - Come on, repeat after me: 'We are both in the same situation; therefore we must be friends - because I am! - Why are you looking at me as if I were a machine gun? Look me in the eye: come on, man! I need you.

(Enormous terror dispalyed by the other inmate who might be mute or just a dense man, and who had been brainwashed by his torturers with some horrific information about DANIIL)

DANIIL: When someone has been alone for such a long time one needs somebody's presence...I have only one true friend: **Schnauzer**. I murdered my wife and daughter, and I was left Schnauzer only. (*Convinced*) **Schnauzer will revenge us**! He is taking part in a dog's competition of paramount importance: **he was** entered **as the property of my little girl, Eva**! - The one I murdered. - When the result of the competition is announced, his photograph together with that of my little girl will be published in all the newspapers of the Planet, it will be broadcast on all the screens of all the TV channels...! Hary prepared a whole set of coloured photographs: Schnauzer at the photographer, Schnauzer running, Schnauzer catching the ball, - on the swing, at the window, on the tricycle, carrying the newspapers... very many...! And others: swimming with Eva, walking with Eva, dancing with Eva...

(*Confession*) Hary has also prepared some photographs of Mara, my wife, who I murdered together with Eva: He promised he would do his best to publicise them! Mara has also got the right, as she is my wife! - To be a little celebrity! - You see none of us enjoyed any happiness from anyone else. We had only the enjoyment we had created for each other... My little girl was excluded from school in her very first day of school: they went on strike, they demonstrated with placards...

(*With immense grief*) Even so don't you want to talk to me? Are you disgusted with me? I have not asked you anything else but to tell me what is the date today!... If you don't want to tell me, so be it! There is nothing I can do! But you must consider that... that we are going to be together here for a long time, and...

(*Immense terror with the other inmate. DANIIL will scrutinize him carefully and he will conclude*)

DANIIL: It is clear that he is in shock. Perhaps it is a scheme ... (*He will point upwards to the spy camera.*) to make me accept. (*He will shout*) But I did not do this for money, I do not need your dirty freedom, I did it to convince you of how hypocritical and evil you are and what pigs you are! Uuuuuah!... I could demolish these walls on you... (*To the new inmate*) Do not be so frightened, damn it: I am not even able to kill the cockroaches, which stole my bread calendar. I reprieved all of them. It is true that, from time to time, I menace them, but I do this to maintain discipline. If I did not do it, you could not even move around here because of them - they are absolutely callous! - Do you like dogs? (*He will recite from Esenin*)

'At dawn… outside a raging storm
A bitch gave birth to seven ginger pups
On golden straw under the haystack
Of the crooked wooden hut.

Bent, watching them until dusk,
She spoiled them and licked them on.
While the drifted snow was melting
On her burning sucked in belly.

In the evening, after the hens had settled,
Morose, the master of the house came out
And threw her seven pups in his bag
As the tormented mother flared mad.

The bitch chased on after the bag behind,
Running onto the snowdrifts in the road…
When the spring water kidnapped her pups
She whined and dript from her muzzle.

Then, when the moon returned unsure
And when she was all alone in her nest
One of the pups appeared as the Moon
Above the house, on the horizon,

And as if someone in the yard, on purpose,
Were to throw a stone instead of bread,
The bitch would cry her sad eyes out
Like big golden stars onto the snow.'

…But do you like people?... You don't want to talk.
Have you come to spy on me? Are you part of their
manipulation plan? (*He will shout to the corner*)
Gentleman cockroaches, don't you come out: we have
an informer amongst ourselves! That is… between you

128

and me! (*To the new inmate*) Look here: if you tell me what day it is today, perhaps we can collaborate - Why are you stuck against that door? Are you hiding something? Turn so I can search you. Turn1 Otherwise I'll smash you!

(*He will turn him by force. The New inmate will prop himself up with his palms against the door. Terrified, DANIIL will retreat: The New inmate's back is the chitin from the back of a huge cockroach, marked with a white line of tooth paste*)

THE NEW INMATE (*with all his might*): Help! He is raping me!

(*Daniil will let himself down, his head in his hands. Two gaolers will enter groaning, and they will beat him ritualistically and with the same movements like in* **Today – In the Evening.** *In the end, one of them will throw an object in the middle of the cell. They will sort out each other's uniform, they will wipe each other's sweat; and then they will leave*)

DANIIL (*in a broken voice ironically*): Lads, do not go!... I have never liked farewells... I am like a rug doll. (*He will move one leg, while resting on his belly.*) The right leg..., good! And the other one is also good. Let's see the hands... They will do! I think that this one is pulled from the shoulder. But it's OK; it still is! It is ah, ah, ah...: the head! I believe it is broken. Am I now like Eva's puppet?... It aches, damn it...! ...Do not swear, you there, rub it!... You swear like a young lad with spots on his face... Damn it, apricot in the milk of life!

(He stands up groaning. He will check the limbs of his body)

DANIIL: A first class job: the craftsmen! I tremble, therefore I exist!... What a nightmare...! Could they have hit me too hard? Or perhaps because... do I talk too much to myself? I talk to the objects, to my memories, that's why... Ho, ho, a cockroach-man, with me in the cell?!... What imagination!... To be or not to be in the real, that's the question for me!

Anyway, why should I be surprised? **I marked the cockroaches**, - those which I warned! With toothpaste! So that... Everything is possible. Finished! Finished because I am losing it! That is... I am climbing up the walls. (*He shouts*) You are not so good!...- Why do I say '*you*'?... Perhaps '*the others*', the ones outside, I don't even know...!? Perhaps it is the Commandant's business only..?! No, of course that they are all guilty: they are interested in profits only!... And what image do you appear to have in other people's eyes! The more evil you commit, the more charitable you show yourself to be; the more lives you put in danger by starving, the more compassionate you show yourselves towards those struck by fate; the more putrid your soul is, the more loving you show yourselves to be... Of the Lord!... - I knew and I let you do your dirty game: with crowns, with bunches of flowers, with children in the cortège carrying their portraits... With your entire families in mourning... With your faces flooded by hypocritical sadness... - After the funeral, you felt relieved: you had not eaten garlic for fear that your breath might smell. But even when you showed yourselves as good Christians: the whole town saw how you wasted your time at the funeral...

- I was prudent, you hypocritical scoundrels: I watched the **comedy of your Christian love** from under the flattened hat of the lame beggar, who was propped up on a metal stick with its end sharpened like a spear.

I let you bury the body of my beloved wife and child there where it was convenient to your charitable vanity, - what does it matter if the grave has a wooden cross or a funerary monument? This was your burial... My burial was different: true, with real tears, with real prayers, with a sworn oath!... I had put them to sleep because of you; I cut a flock of their hair and I cut a flock of my hair, I mixed mine with theirs and I asked for their forgiveness. Before giving myself up, I entered the church where I used to go with Mara during religious festivals and I buried the hair in the frame of Our Lady's icon. - **This is their sacred burial, my burial undertaken for them**! They deserved it, because...they died for you! I have wronged, but I wronged for you. By making them martyrs! Though I don't love you at all...

(Someone confused or with intention, has thrown a radio set into the rubbish skip, which, though bitten by a rat, begins to play the tune 'The Evening before Tomorrow')

DANIIL (*will be surprised, then delighted, he will let himself carried away by the rhythm of the music.*): If I were ever to be released, I shall never search for them where you had taken them! (*Dancing*) We are together, in Our Lady's bosom and if I were to go to them, that's where I shall go: to give them news. (*Almost happy*)

Oh, divine apricot tree
That calls at Saturnalias

131

Alone in the Forum
I celebrate
The horizon is preparing
Funerals at sunset
For the passing
Into the natural fruit…

(He will dance until exhausted: until a new transport of garbage will disturb the accidentally triggered apparatus)

DANIIL (*exhausted*): Such divine music is generated by the wretched refuse bins!... Ha, ha, ha, I am relaxed… I remain so furious and strung up after they beat me…! It shouldn't happen. It damages my nerves. It also spoils my digestion… But if they do their utmost to wind me up?!... I should react more calmly. As long as I know that the truth is on my side, I should react in a superior manner. I have only decided and I shudder at the thought that I could resemble them. - I watched on television how an old man was running through Sarajevo with a cloth bag in hand. One could see that the bag was heavy. He was running away from death! But he did not throw his bag because he was perhaps thinking that he would need it again, if he were to escape with his life. …I believe that I retained this as a parabola: the old man had three possibilities: *die from shooting*, - if they got him, *die of hunger*, - if he were to lose his food bag, *die of old age*, - if they missed him and if he saved his bag! He was facing the possibility of choosing his own death - all certain, and in an almost near future. But he did not want to choose it, he was running away: he was running away! He was deluding himself, and the television was deluding its audience about the old man who was running away from his own death! No, he was running away from the horror of choosing…! It is, a…! A knife?!...

(He prudently looked at the door, then at the spy camera. He pretended to be concerned with cleaning his nostrils - into which he eagerly put his fingers - as he advanced undetected, silently moving his soles along the floor and with his back to the camera. After he reassured himself that he had hidden the knife with his body, he began to eagerly perform a gymnastics exercise ending up with genuflexions. He took the knife, quite a big and impressive object, he scrutinized it while he continued his exercise with only one hand, jumping - he hid the knife under his twilled cloth coat. Then he stopped)

DANIIL: What a sensation of power it gives me!?... And of security! (*He is feeling it under his twilled cloth coat.*) What a pleasant coolness!... Hm, yes… it is sharp. Good… good…! Damn it, keeping it next to my skin, I am experiencing a frisson as if I have become twice a man on the spot! - (*Overwhelmed*) Am I not fearful any longer?!... Am I not fearful any more of… them?!... (*He would become provocative*) With you, I can modify objects into useful things anytime and beings into throw-away-corpses…! I understand why you are venerated: cutting the umbilical cord, which still holds the baby to its mother made you become the father of life. (*Gesticulating with the knife*) You… lighten! You split! You cut up, you divide and sever: you are a god, I understand! And a friend. I shall give you a name: you are called… you are called… (He is making a visible effort to find a name) I cannot succeed. I have never succeeded. And Eva: when she was born, I saw she was alive and… I knew that Eva means life and I called her: Eva. I bought her a parrot and when she asked me about its name, I was unable to tell her that it had a different name than... Parrot, as it had been created by our Lord!... Our pedigree dog Schnauzer is called Schnauzer, therefore... I shall call you: Knife! Like your name. Amen! (*To himself*) I cannot give it a name, because I cannot lie on any account: the name never tells the truth. '...Andrei: brave, courageous!..' And Andrei... he poos on himself, fearing his boss might dismiss him!... – 'Luca: bright!...' And Luca... shines murdering children's souls!...- 'David: loved!...' And David... is the very Commandant of this gaol! Could one find one's way out of so many lies? Could one/ set oneself free from/ so many/ lies?... (*Suddenly, he will call accusingly*) Hey, you, come here and take your bait! Who has left it here? (*He will run in a fit of madness*) That psychopath, whom you wanted to indict?... Stupid people!... Or the gaolers? That wants to say: another crime: I took away the bayonet! Yes? How many days will you add to my solitary confinement, oi, you, subtle-stupid? Apricot and mother's milk of clever-pooers!... (*He will observe a cockroach, he will kneel and, with all his strength, he will hit it with the knife on the floorboards*) Haven't I told you I don't want to catch you? (*He will hit again*) Haven't I cautioned you? (*He will hit and, almost fainting, he will shout while following the cockroach on his knees towards the corner of the cell*) What methods should I still use? How should I behave? How can I communicate with you, and with you, and with you, and with you, and with you? Damn you stay still! You can manage... You can manage. You can manage...! (*He will let the cockroach fall in its hole. He will howl with fury, he will stand up*) You can all manage but me...!

(He *will raise the knife with both hands, to stab himself in the chest*)

DANIIL (*He screams*): Aaaah…!
A VOICE: Now!... (*Short pause*)
DANIIL (*a slight laughter replaces his scream and shakes his body.*): Ha, ha, ha, ha…! Have you also thought of this situation!... Father's idiots, idiots!... You said to yourselves that… perhaps… I shall commit suicide?... **I have not managed to learn anything**. (*He will kneel*) Hey, Old Man, Old Man Lord!... (*He will throw the knife towards the door*) We need so little to be happy and we make superhuman efforts to make unhappy those who should be our nearest and dearest! (*He will recite*) 'Curse be the land for you: thorns and horse thistle for you to sprout; you will eat your bread onto the sweat of your face, until you will return to the earth from which you had been taken; because you are the earth and you will turn into earth.'

You are continuously trying us, you are sending us new diseases, more terrible every time, so that you can see for yourself, - and be surprised once again! -, that can we manage… Then, if we still manage, you send us other more dreadful illnesses! But Lord, until when? **Aren't you tired of punishing us on and on**? Because we don't get tired of suffering, Lord, - You will better abandon us to our devices! When I did what I did, I tried to pacify you: I sacrificed my darlings Mara and Eva for you, I did it to support your teachings: so that people can see! - Why don't you do it so that seeing this, they could become better people?... I remained here to suffer alone, and I shall suffer until the end, for you too! - Show me a sign and bring peace amongst people on Earth.

Old Man, we need so little to be happy!...

I was happy a few times. You know too: (*He will count on his fingers*) when I got married; when Eva was born; when I was offered a home; when Eva was singing a duet with a boy and she closed his unzipped fly at the pre-school celebrations; when Eva poured my first linden tea and when she sweetened it with honey... That's about all. Eight times. I needed, oh Lord, to be happy only twice or three times more, and that would have been enough: I would have come to you as the most content amongst the content persons. Now, do not be angry, Old Man, I wish to have only one more satisfaction: to achieve togetherness through my suffering, to unite against the dreadful disease, which you had sent us! You owe me this one! Do not say that I fight against you! - I fight for your teachings Old Man; forgive me, but it seems to me that to you punishment has become more important than alienation! (*He will make the sign of the cross.*) Amen! (*He will stand up lively and emaciated*) Oi, why don't you come back so that I can return the poison? If it hasn't worked out already!... Modernise yourselves because Europe will not accept you, you..., intelligent shits!...

(*He will stop: a memory! His face will lighten up, and he will burst into laughter*)

DANIIL: As Mara was saying!... I remember...! Ha, ha, ha, ha!... the intelligent shit from next door! Our neighbour... Our neighbour, an intelligent shit with a goatee and... very sexy...! Ha, ha, ha, ha!... Hidden by Mara in the bathroom, stunned, Hary and I were listening/; 'Mrs Mara, I have been fighting with you for two months: I had enough!' – 'Please, let's help

136

ourselves to this chocolate, please'. – 'I don't need anything, Madam...!' – 'But the chocolate is an aphrodisiac...Otherwise I cannot!..." – 'If you insist... Hasn't it got a strange taste?' – 'Now drink some peach nectar.' – 'This, yes! It is very good and it is cold...' – 'Finish this tablet too...' The cretin was stuffing himself with laxatives, like in a hospital – 'Let's sit down. Only a little...!' 'But, Mrs Mara...I...' – 'Mr Mincu...' – 'Call me Teo!' 'OK Teo I go to the bathroom to change. You... get undressed...!' - Ha, ha, ha, ha!... When Mara gave us the sink plunger and the meat cleaver in hand, and she pushed us into the bedroom... ho, ho, ho!... the intelligent shit was farting!...He ran in his underpants, farting so loud that the walls were shaking! Hi, hi, hi, hi, hoh! - Mara was shouting, throwing his clothes out of the window: 'Go collect your clothes! Get out, obsessed sicko!...' - I did not beat him. We made fun of him that was all! Mara said she had enough. She was very kind-hearted... Or, how was she? To have my glasses made was more important to her than the War in Yugoslavia. This was happening far away and was, naturally, less important than her family; it was not worth any commentary, because, more important things were happening close by: 'DANIIL, Momiță the crook has postponed the photosensitive lenses yet again! How will you manage with your red eyes this winter?' - As a matter of fact Hary is also extremely considerate: 'Be economic with the truth and you will have less problems: smile and say... only a fraction: a small slice, so small, so small. The less you say the least mistakes you make! I have always said this to you: keep your mouth in control and make big steps and you will reach far and well! And I have also said to you: it's not the cold, which is bitter, but it is the coat, which is thin! - Don't you also wish to be happy?, - happiness is in the deep understanding of life!... Now you can swear at me: I have nothing left to say!' (*Mean*) I informed the authorities that there is a conspiracy from everybody against my uncertainty: everyone wants something; even the laws force me to be happy, or... to appear to be happy. I am asked to be good and compassionate: to understand everybody without being understood - I do not trust them! Old Man, Old Lord! You know how much Mara was boring me; you know how I was so fed up with Hary, when they were forcing me to be happy. But only Eva and Schnauzer saved me from running away. A terrible spleen languishes in the world: primary school teachers, secondary school teachers, priests of all denominations; doctors, drivers, waiters; academics, parliamentarians, ministers, presidents - all earn their living offering me happiness. Even my kidneys and my veins are carefully transporting liquids so that I am healthy in order that I can enjoy complete happiness. (*As above :*) A hymn emerges in my cells each time when I get up healthy. - Old Man, you have given me so many possibilities to be happy...! Combinations of five multiplied by 'n', in which 'five' is the number of senses and 'n' is the number of life forms... and of inanimate forms... on the earth... but I, Old Man, I am bored. I only want to be left alone. I am only interested in myself: to see myself, to smell myself, to hear myself, to taste myself, to touch myself - unknown and alone! - to understand myself, Old Lord! It is the only form of happiness that I wish for. Old Man, save me from evil, from this Universe you made and which disgusts me because it is using me without my knowledge: for what? And I do not understand: for what purpose? It is not fair, Lord, to have fun by creating the world and then, by leaving it to us to wash our hands with it!

(The hall will shake because of the heaps of rubbish: the specific jolting of the rubbish refuse toboggan will be heard and again, it will rain over the audience with bits of paper, scraps of fur, textiles, bits of polystyrene and lots and lots of newspapers. In a few places, big cloth puppets impersonating clowns, poor people, and clerks will be left hanging.)

DANIIL: The refuse skip has been filled up... Light, heat and stench come from its direction...! There is my place, there I am expected - when I reach it, I shall be peaceful. I was so sure that **I did good when I did what I did**!... Now, I am not so sure... I feel how discouragement is seizing me... My doubt is guilty of all my fears. In my dream, dear Mara begs me not to kill my child; in my dream, darling Eva covers Mara's mouth with her palms: 'Don't give it to her! Don't give it to her! Don't give it to her!!...'. She is guarding her from me, so that she won't drink the poison, and she herself smothers her out of fear and too much love! More often, in my dream, both fall on their knees and implore me to let them... to taste... the bitter life... a few more days at least... Lord, I should not have sinned!? I was hurt the most! I atone for it and I gladly welcome my suffering! Alone, I provoked my punishment for which my henchmen had not dreamt even in their sleep! - I am not a hero. It is not true that I wanted and that I wished to be another Jesus of self-sacrifice! I wished, Lord, only... that my mistake be a sign! - If I was haughty, forgive me... *(With devotion)* And Lord help Schnauzer win! Hary will take care that Mara and Eva re-enter the world next to him with their wonderful faces resting on his silver fur... they will spread happiness and confidence amongst people! - When I gave myself up and I showed their photographs to the police, a lieutenant fainted - they were so beautiful.

Once I hit a bolder, which had fallen into the road. Due to inertia, I bent over the stirring wheel. Mara got out of her seat to grab me. (*Scream*) Have you understood? I was the most important person in the world! She hit her head and she sprained her hand trying to protect me... (*Sobs*) She cared for me, she loved me..., - I only wanted to help them!... I only wanted to revenge them!... I wanted to make you become what you had said **you would have liked to be**! - And I do not get anything else... but turn myself into what I see that **you are already** in this reality.

A VOICE: Attention! (*DANIIL stands to attention.*) Come in front of the camera. (*An unclear image will appear on the screen.*) Come closer. (*DANIIL will come closer. An enormous cockroach will be contoured on the screen, while the light will abate*) Smile. Number.

DANIIL's Voice: 4979!

THE VOICE: How do you feel?

THE COCKROACH (*with Daniil's voice: metallic, dense, as if read from a recording at a lower speed than normal*) I feel ex-cel-lent, as you wish!

A VOICE: Are you pleased with the regime of detention?

THE COCKROACH (*with DANIIL's voice read at an even slower speed*): I-t i-s e-x-c-e-l-l-e-n-t!

The VOICE: I don't understand what you wish to demonstrate!?... Four days of solitary confinement will be added to your punishment. You will spend a total of 35 days here. For the time being!

THE COCKROACH: (*Unintelligible sounds of prehistoric animal*)

The VOICE: Are you pleased with the regime of detention?

THE COCKROACH: (*Similar sounds like those experienced in an immense grotto when filled and emptied by an enormous wave*)

The VOICE: Excellent. You are left with the same 35 days of solitary confinement. You have 10 extra days.

THE COCKROACH: (*The same, like the groan of a triggered avalanche*)

A VOICE: In the corner. March. (*The cockroack turns towards the screen. It has its back marked with a white line.*) To bed!... Everybody is content, nobody wants anything. It is... Lights out...!

(*It is dark*)

A VOICE (*similar to an announcement at a railway station*): Leave the hall!... Leave the hall!... Do not applaud! Leave the hall!... Let the judges enter!... Let the judges enter!... (*Uniformed males and females appear from the sides of the stage; they wear the helmets of shield bearers, with shields of Plexiglas and enormous paintbrushes with white tips*) Leave the hall!... Leave the hall!... (*The audience is led out of the hall in semi-darkness*) Leave the hall!... Do not applaud, leave the hall!... (*The audience is led out of the hall by the dustbins*) Leave the hall!... Leave the hall!...

If it can be ended,
The End

141

THE OLD LADY AND THE THIEF
(Bătrâna şi Hoțul)[4]

Characters:

THE OLD LADY
THE THIEF
THE FIRST CIVILIAN
THE SECOND CIVILIAN
ANTON

The action happens in the house of the person who believed that happiness could not be anything else but mere

---

[4] **Printed in the volumes:** *„Jocul de dincolo de ploaie"*, P.H. Junimea, Iaşi, 1985; *„Pagini alese de Petre Isachi"*, P.H. Plumb, Bacău, 2000; *„Doamne, fă ca Schnauzer să câştige!"*, P.H. Casa Scriitorilor, Bacău, 2004.
Performed at: Dramatic Theatre „Bacovia", Bacău, theatrical seasons 1984-1988, director Mircea Marin; „Teatrul Mic", Bucureşti, theatrical seasons 1987-1989 and 1991-1992, director Cristian Hadjiculea; Dramatic Theatre „Al. Davila", Piteşti, theatrical season 1990-1991, director Al. Zărnescu; Dramatic Theatre „Ovidiu", Constanţa, theatrical season 1991-1992, director Dan Alecsandrescu; „Mihai Eminescu" Theatre, Botoşani, theatrical season 1997-1998, director Marius Rogojinschi; Radio Iaşi, „Teatru la microfon", april 1998, director Marius Rogojinschi; TVR National Theatre, „TVR – Cultural", „TVR – Internaţional", director Olimpia Arghir (starring Irina Răchiţeanu and Sorin Medeleni), 13 times broadcasted only between 1991 and 2000; „Teatrul Valah", Giurgiu, theatrical season 2004-2005, director Mircea Creţu; „G.A. Petculescu" Theatre, Reşiţa, theatrical season 2009-2010, director Iustina Prisăcaru.

harmony between a being and the existence one leads. This definition appeared empty to his wife - but though, fearful and ill fated, she did not wish to die.

The scene represents a spacious room, which has massive doors to the left and to the right. The entrance to the WC stands concealed by a velvet curtain on the wall to the left. There is a window on the wall to the right.

The walls are covered in fine paintings dominated by browns and yellows. There are nudes, portraits of a man painted in various positions - probably the painter himself - and roses. The painting on the centre wallat at the back is outstanding; it portrays a young lady caught in movement, with her chest towards the onlooker, her face lit by a discreet smile and her shining neck straight, under thick hair. It is a perfect drawing. The colour had been applied with great skill to emphasise the shapes. The frame, covered in gold leaf, shows that the owners treasure this painting.

It is rather late at night.

Rays of light from car lights brush the room. Car noises and sometimes the clear movement of car wheels give dimension to the desolation of the night.

The window is suddenly filled in with the shadow of a man who is trying to break in. He succeeds. He behaves prudently: he listens and he moves with caution. His movements are precise.

The telephone rings abruptly. He covers it with his hands, as if trying to smother it. The telephone continues to ring stridently. Maddened, THE THIEF takes out a knife and he hits the cable between the box and the receiver, cutting it. Silence. THE THIEF breathes heavily, one hand on the telephone and one hand on the knife.

A noise can be heard coming from the door onto the left. An Old Lady enters carrying a burning candle in one hand. There are about 30 centimetres left from her wedding candle. THE THIEF hides behind the curtains of the window.

THE OLD LADY: How many times have I asked them to repair my lighting and they tell me there are no funds. On the other hand, Ifrim is not a specialist. He is not qualified! He appears qualified when he is tipsy every day. (*She switches on the light. She lifts the receiver.*) Hello! Hello! Hello!... The receiver is dead. At this hour! To inconvenience people and to prevent them from using it. Someone must have realised he had dialled the wrong number... but, anyway, he could have thought that somebody might have been woken up in the middle of the night and that this person deserves an apology! Someone in a hurry... Hello! Hello!... (*She blows into the receiver*) I haven't even got a dialling tone! You've woken me up! I wish you to have my sleep. (*She walks away the candle in one hand and the receiver in her other hand. She tries to switch off the light with the hand in which she is holding the receiver; she cannot do it*) If I were two years younger, I would repair it all by myself. I would venture it; all is to make a start... I go round with all sorts of things. Old age is taking its toll! (*She puts the receiver inside the pocket of her dressing gown and she switches off the light*) At least, I haven't forgotten. Now I must close the door and let them know that it's all nonsense and that everything is broken inside here because all is so old that it lets the draft in and because here I am not even allowed to light a fire at night...

(*The old lady leaves the room, and closes the door behind her. The Thief appears from behind the curtains, he listens, and he walks towards the wall at the back from where he takes off the painting already described. Noises can be heard from behind the door on the left.*)

145

The Old Lady opens it. She is carrying the burning candle and the telephone receiver. The Thief puts the painting down, leans it against the wall, and he hides behind the curtains)

THE OLD LADY *(entering)*: Tomorrow, I shall repair the door myself. With a screwdriver and a bit of plaster. I shall repair it and call them to see that I do not need their assistance: I can manage on my own, without any bureaucracy. (*She switches on the light*) How could I have broken the wire without realising it!?... Perhaps it weakened somewhere, and when I pulled... (*She laughs*) To walk away with the receiver!... Bravo! At least, let's not mention it. (*She puts down the receiver. Then she stares away. She lifts the receiver, as if she has woken from a dream*) Yes! Hello! Yes! Please... Tell me... Again... (*She puts down the receiver, she looks at the telephone and she bursts out laughing. She takes a serious pose for a moment, she lifts up the receiver once again, and she speaks*) And please do not call again! The receiver is out of order. I broke the cable and I cannot hear you. I can only hear it ring, and it is not normal to be woken up in the middle of the night! There!... (*She slams down the receiver and she laughs*) I told him!... (*She laughs*) If someone were to see me, he might think I am having fun!... No... An Old Lady is a serious person, regarding death, it makes her very wise, blasé and serious: she does not do superfluous things. No! (*She stands up; she sees the painting, which is leaning against the wall*) Oh my Lord! It has fallen! (*She blows the candle out, she puts it on the table, and she walks in the direction of the painting*) It is not broken! Oh my Lord, it is good nothing happened to it, my dear painting! A miracle of a painting! How did that drunken Ifrim hang it up? I'll scold them tomorrow!... All of them! (*The Thief*

146

comes out of his hiding - The Old Lady looks around her)
I did not donate all my treasures, so that they could mock
at them!. (*She sees him*) And why are you standing there
like a wooden pole? Come and help me. Can't you see I
am unable to lift it? (*The Thief comes nearer and he lifts
the painting*) Put it on the table... Move away from it,
you are all useless. Like the butterflies; beautiful and...
that is all! Nevertheless, tell me: how did you get in?

THE THIEF: Through the window.

THE OLD LADY: I do not like bad jokes. Now, that I have
already let you in, tell me what brings you here.
Nevertheless, you must know that I cannot solve
anything. You must go to the office tomorrow. (...) Good
evening! Please! (*She points to the door*)

THE THIEF: I am sorry Madam that we don't understand
one another: I entered through the window, and you are
so senile that you don't realise anything. I witnessed the
entire circus with the telephone; Sit yourself down on
this chair (*He helps her to sit down*) until I finish my job.

THE OLD LADY: As far as I understand, you are... - if I
am wrong, please excuse me: you are a, a...

THE THIEF: A Thief, Madam!

THE OLD LADY: And aren't you ashamed to say it?

THE THIEF: Not at all, Madam! (...) What a beautiful
painting.

THE OLD LADY: My portrait... My husband was awarded
the silver medal at the Paris International Exhibition in
1935.

THE THIEF: It's worth it.

THE OLD LADY: You said that I am senile and that I am
not aware of anything.

THE THIEF: I regret, but I like to be clear.

THE OLD LADY: However, I realise that you are on the
point of committing a crime.

THE THIEF: This proves that you are not completely senile: my condolences!

(A short pause)

THE OLD LADY: What is the reason for your 'Condolences'?

THE THIEF: Because you're completely mad!

(A short pause)

THE OLD LADY: You wanted to crack a joke, or you do not know what 'condolences' mean?

THE THIEF: Condolences... that is, congratulations.

THE OLD LADY: Condolences are passed on to somebody who had a death in the family.

THE THIEF: It's all the same; it's all the same!

THE OLD LADY: However, a gentleman, an art Thief should expect more from oneself.

THE THIEF: Nothing can be done, Old Lady! My true culture is my lack of culture...

THE OLD LADY: You are behaving forbiddingly insulting!

THE THIEF: Without any effort, I promise you!

(He studies the painting)

THE OLD LADY: What a pity: you are intelligent.

THE THIEF: Ta...

THE OLD LADY: You succeeded in tricking the alarm system too!

THE THIEF (*stands stone still. He puts the painting on the table*) Which system?

THE OLD LADY: The alarm system. Because it is extremely valuable, the painting is protected by special technical apparata!

THE THIEF (*he lets himself down on a chair, he wipes his forehead with his hand*) I'd be damned!

THE OLD LADY: By now, you should have been arrested a long time ago…! (*She stands up and she walks towards the empty space on the wall*)

THE THIEF: Do not move! (*He rushes and he holds her by the arm*)

THE OLD LADY: This little box, can you see it? It should have sounded the alarm when you lifted the painting. Perhaps it is blocked! Would you like to check what is wrong with it?

THE THIEF: Oh Lord, and I can't even slap you!... Damn you, go back to your place when I ask you!... You'll drive me mad if nothing else!

THE OLD LADY (*pushed to the chair*): You cannot really believe that you will leave with this painting! I must do something to prevent you… Why don't you want to help me?

THE THIEF (*stares at her*): Look: I'll help you if you help me. OK?

THE OLD LADY: You are a nice boy.

THE THIEF: For the time being, let's establish a few facts: you don't get nearer that wall, you don't leave - without my permission - the chair on which you are sitting, and you don't try to run away… And, in general, you don't try anything on. Agreed?

THE OLD LADY: Agreed. Moreover, I should not phone the police.

THE THIEF (*distrustful*): You're clever…! OK.

THE OLD LADY: In exchange, put the painting back on the wall and leave. Tomorrow, I expect to drink coffee with you. However, if you are not in a hurry now…!

Ifrim will put the painting back. He will also check the alarm system... (*She is trying to stand up. The Thief is making her sit down*) If the alarm works, you realize that we cannot talk any longer.

THE THIEF: The matter is: if you don't calm down, I'll tie you up!

THE OLD LADY (*dumbfounded*): Do not do such a thing!

THE THIEF: On the contrary, I'll do it! Look... (He takes out a rope)

THE OLD LADY: Then two crimes are being committed, stealing a painting and tying up an Old Lady...

THE THIEF: Shut up!

(*The Thief takes out a patent, a screwdriver - he takes the canvas out of its frame. Car noises. Somewhere, engine noise.*)

THE OLD LADY: Will you handle the canvas carefully, please? One works with care in a museum... I have taken the painting in custody and... (*The Thief silences her with a gesture: he is working. After a while, she says*) I would like to speak.

THE THIEF: If you can say something normally! And not a lot.

THE OLD LADY: You might not know this, but you find yourself in a memorial house...

THE THIEF: I know: Nicu Arin's!

THE OLD LADY: Then, you might be surprised to learn that I donated it to the state with everything inside here, including the building! Set at a value of almost two million.

THE THIEF: I'm not surprised. People do all sort of weird things after they reach a certain age.

THE OLD LADY: He was a great painter! I had to accept the sacrifice. He succeeded in achieving what many have never succeeded in doing... He was an honest man... Every one of his paintings was a joy and people need joy. His paintings speak the same language to everybody and they try to make people feel better and more sensitive... That's why I've given everything away (...) With the risk of living only of the pitiful meagre pension of an art teacher... Fully aware, I faced the risk of travelling only once with the master's paintings and only where they were requested... He created wonderful paintings! He suffered a lot, because he loved his work enormously... He was a painter whom the painters themselves punished because of his love for the art of painting!

THE THIEF (*he had taken the canvas down and he admires it*): What do you say about this, it's a certificate of quality. I'll double the price!

THE OLD LADY: I thought that I'd make you understand.

THE THIEF: Look for somebody else!...

(*A short pause*)

THE OLD LADY: However, so that you could leave with something, I suggest you replace it.

THE THIEF: What should I replace?

THE OLD LADY: The painting. I shall give you another one in its place. I still have some paintings, which I have not donated to the state. I kept them, because... Because... they were painted especially for me...!

THE THIEF (*stares at her*): The truth is you haven't given me a headache. I like you and that's why... I regret, but this is the painting, which was ordered!

THE OLD LADY: By whom?

THE THIEF (*menacing*): Well, take it easy! (*Raising his voice*) Don't take me for an idiot when I speak to you and I'll treat you humanely, otherwise I'll change my tune! Then I'll allow you to grumble... Damn you, why

151

aren't you asleep at this hour? Why do you confuse me? Well, well do not be afraid, I'm not so horrible. Have you been younger, I'd have tied you up and I'd have gagged you; have you been a man, I'd have broken your neck. So there, you see: you are lucky.

THE OLD LADY: I am sorry for you, but… I am honestly saying that you will not take the painting!

THE THIEF: OK. I see that I'll have to tie you up in the end.

THE OLD LADY: You'll be unable to take it. Because it's unconceivable: The painter's masterpiece cannot be missing from His historic home. From this institution! My annulment!

THE THIEF: So much? Than it's exactly what I must do.

THE OLD LADY: I am tired, but I ask you to think that you'll be unable to leave with this painting!

THE THIEF: You're mad, love.

THE OLD LADY: I am not forcing you to apologize. Perhaps, with you, this phrase… is street elegance…

THE THIEF (*roars with unstoppable laughter. He chokes, he stops, he laughs again*): Listen… listen… listen, you intellectual one!... (*He laughs*) Be careful: I'd be damned if I ever have met a more insolent daring person than you! (*He laughs.*) I ask you to lock me up if there's something alike in the rest of Europe, and I'll tell you that I've seen everything: You don't give up. You hold it with your teeth…(...). That's why I like you. But I can't change it: you must bear it!... (*He stops laughing as if hit in the face. The change from the roar of laughter to the scream of anger happens all of a sudden.*) Because you're a stinky one! Like all of them!... Don't open your mouth because I'll break it, do you hear me? I might be a Thief, but I know what fairness means. Perhaps just because of this! (*He breathes out menacingly*) My father worked, he fought with danger… you carried yourselves like snakes, hidden, tamed, nobody had expected you... and, suddenly, you bit!... He was thrown overboard just when he was doing his best. You turned him back from where he had started, and you... You succeeded. Again, you awarded yourselves high wages, you had books published, and you travelled and relaxed. And memorial houses! You were the enemies...! You must know that you are unable to see the cloth scribbled like in bourgeois times because, nowadays, it praises you instead of punishing you! Who asks for it, knows what they are up to!

THE OLD LADY: I only wish to point out that you are irreverent...

THE THIEF: You're looking down on me. I wipe my derrière with your scorn, because I've also read books! You should learn that for the first time in my life I'm proud of what I'm doing. Because I do it justice!

THE OLD LADY: Name what you wish for, whatever it is you're doing. It is clear you are doing it for the money.

THE THIEF: Justice is also paid for in this world!

THE OLD LADY: You are so strung up, as if you were certain you were eternal... It is enough to wish for what is possible only in order to become content. Artists are wise: they know that all those who persecute them will disappear, but art... Art is eternal! For ever... (...) You may starve a people; you may lock up many of them; you may divide them into two; one group may oppress the other group... But nobody, can ever burn their eyes, break their eardrums, and scoop their brains, for the simple reason that it is not possible... The Roman emperors had declared themselves gods and they had statues and paintings made to order for them; thus they tried - they knew it was the only way - to fight oblivion. Through art! What have they left? Ridicule! And an immense roar of laughter! Statues and the paintings disappeared… Because they were not art… They were only a dull and lamentable 'fear'. That's why! Do you understand?

THE THIEF (*after a pause*): Anyway, I still have a grudge against you. In spite of all this… I also like art: sometimes, especially when I feel inclined, and I am confident - when I am joyful and alone and when I walk in the street, it is as if I have generators in my joints. In all my joints; They vibrate and always push me forward and I walk, and, as I walk, I want to walk more, and I don't see the people around me and I suddenly find myself on the outskirts of the town: in the fields. There, I feel my feet weak and I sit down. I become one with the earth! Something is struggling in my chest: something warm and soft, but every time more alive and I know that I haven't lived this one. That is to say, that I have lived it, but every time in a different way… This is art, isn't it?

THE OLD LADY: This was what my husband was feeling when he was painting…

(*A short pause*)

THE THIEF: Now, you must not believe that you have tricked me and that I should not finish my business.

(*He stands up and he brings a Hessian cloth from behind the curtains in order to wrap up the painting*)

THE OLD LADY: Tomorrow, I could pay you the sum promised by the person who had ordered you to steal the painting. I have some money in the bank. If that is not enough…

THE THIEF: I explained to you that this isn't a matter of money only. When this house came into being, 'by royal appointment', many heads fell: because they committed

154

abuse, because they weren't in step with the times, because of... All sorts of things! Now they are living from hand to mouth and Nicu Arin has a house all to himself even in death?! Is it because Carol II touched his forehead? Or is it because Queen Mărioara called him to Yugoslavia to open an exhibition in the Royal Palace in '34? Or is it because he proudly wandered in your company through Macedonia, Montenegro, Dalmatia, Rome, Venice, - I know everything! - , While here, others were working hard, dreaming of a whiter bread?!... And when they finally got it, you raised your head and you snatched it from their hands!... If I think clearly, what an immense danger to order is hidden in art...! In any type of art! The better it is, the more dangerous it is! And surely that artists, - from wherever they might originate -, are some stinky subversives on whom no one can ever rely; because they work alone in their small workshops, and they think! They suddenly appear with some creation in the public domain, and, out of common sense, one cannot destroy it because it is 'true art'. And they start collecting: one today, another one tomorrow, and those who believed that their time had arrived, those who sacrificed themselves, those who created the right conditions - are swept aside. Then one of them emerges when one doesn't even expect!

THE OLD LADY: It is the normal evolution of the world.

THE THIEF: This 'normal' evolution will finally end!

(*He snatches the canvas, and rolls it with nervous gestures*)

THE OLD LADY: Please! Please, handle it with care: it is an exceptionally valuable work...!

THE THIEF: You haven't understood anything!

THE OLD LADY: Do me a favour: allow me to wrap it up! (*She walks towards him with her hands stretched*)

THE THIEF (*long look at her*): All right! After this, you calm down. (*He hands her the canvas.*) Yes… quickly!

THE OLD LADY (*takes the canvas, stretches it, like a farewell*): I was looking like this: I was slender, beautiful!... I had black heavy, black hair and big eyes!... How much we loved each other…(…). I loved being courted… (*She speaks with someone from the past*) 'My dear, I love my husband!...' (*To someone else*) 'You are charming, much more interesting than my husband, but I cannot cheat on him…!' (*She laughs*) 'Very funny on your part!... You are virile: you eat a lot heartily you are sensual. I am attracted to you, but… I shall never cheat on him!...' (*To The Thief*) I like holding my hand to be kissed. I applied a special hygiene to my hands, I would stretch my body when a man bowed and kissed my velvety skin; I felt that life was wonderful…! But I didn't know it was transient. (*Looking at the painting, as if in conversation*) Why do you make useless and dangerous things… when you know we are transient?...

THE THIEF (*who has gathered his tools*): What are you going on about?

THE OLD LADY: It seemed to me that I was so tiny and fragile… And besides this… I loved to dance! (*She is humming a waltz. She swings, she rotates - the scene must be build up without hurry, with affection*)

THE THIEF: You, stand still!

THE OLD LADY (*she sings while she is slowly rotating*): …Do you like dancing? (*She sings.*) To feel strong arms… Holding me… (*She sings*)

THE THIEF: Stop it at once, lunatic! Oi!...

THE OLD LADY (*she is quickly rotating: she is in a hurry*): To feel light, to fly…

THE THIEF (*rushes to stop her*): Damn you!

THE OLD LADY: ...to fly...! To escape...! To fly...! To escape...! (*She stumbles in front of the door to her room and... she falls*)

THE THIEF: Damn it. What are you doing? (*He snatches the canvas from her hand, he looks at it, and he carries it to the table. The Old Lady is crying on the floor.*) You are behaving like a lunatic! Come here and sit on a chair. (*He helps her to stand up*)

THE OLD LADY (*as if she were apologizing*): I wanted to run away, but I did not succeed!

THE THIEF: I saw it!

THE OLD LADY: I am too old to succeed: what can I do?

THE THIEF: To come to terms with it.

THE OLD LADY: It is not right. You are young! I cannot stop you! Do you understand my drama?

THE THIEF (*to himself*) Oh Lord, what have you put me through!

THE OLD LADY (*she moves away*): However, allow me to wrap it up! I implore you!... Masterpieces have a special regime when transported and you do not know how to do it!

THE THIEF (*is throwing the Hessian bag in her face*): Here it is!... And you must know that you didn't even open the door when I almost turned you into an angel. (*He shows the knife to her*) I was going to stub you right into your humpback, do you understand? (*While he puts back the knife*) This, to make us understood in the future!

(*A short pause*)

THE OLD LADY (*she is scared. She makes an effort to control herself. She puts the canvas on the table*): A painting must not be directly wrapped up in Hessian cloth - especially if the cloth, excuse me, is also dirty... No, do not get annoyed: I'll finish immediately!... I have

157

something more suitable... (*She opens a drawer from the chest of drawers and she takes some white paper out*) This is the right paper! (*She walks towards the table and she handles the paper. There is a persistent and irritating noise in the air, which annoys him, and which is clearly getting THE THIEF out of his mind*)

THE THIEF (*makes haste, he places both his hands over the paper, he screams*): Handle it gently!

THE OLD LADY (*scared*): Please, I have not done anything wrong!

THE THIEF: The noise of the paper is digging into my bones! It is drying me out!

THE OLD LADY: It gives me goose bumps: I also cannot stand it. (*At last, she finishes the parcel, wrapping it in the Hessian cloth*) Here you have it! With one condition only!

THE THIEF (*takes the rolled canvas and places it on the table*): There, sit down on a chair and let's say goodbye. (*He pushes her down on the chair*)

THE OLD LADY: Are you going to kill me?

THE THIEF: If I haven't done it until now, it will be pointless at the end! (*He takes the rope out.*) Place your hands on your lap and sit still so that I can tie you up. I'm turning you into a baby, be good (*He ties her to the chair*)

THE OLD LADY: I let you go on one condition only.

THE THIEF (*laughs, moving his head negatively*): You're extraordinary! (*He laughs*)

THE OLD LADY: ...If you give me your word that you'll be careful and the painting will not be damaged. And that it will not be lost...

THE THIEF (*reassures himself that she is well tied up. He takes the rolled canvas and stares at her*)

THE OLD LADY: Please!...

THE THIEF (*gets nearer*): You've got tears in your eyes… (*He touches her face*) You're a bit mad…!

THE OLD LADY: Please!...

THE THIEF (*sighs*): All right! (*He bursts out laughing*) You've got my word of honour. (*He roars with laughter, he stops all of a sudden: he softly taps her face with his palm*) You're extraordinary! (*He leans suddenly*) Moreover, I promise you something else: if that client… doesn't cough up the money as we had agreed, I'll bring it back to you. Upon my word of honour! (*He slaps her gently. He switches off the light.*)

THE OLD LADY: Thank you very much! I trust you. Since I had the pleasure of making your acquaintance, you made a good impression on me from the very beginning…

(*The Thief opens the curtains. Suddenly, the noise of an ambulance can be heard in the street*)

THE THIEF (*leaps back. He screams hysterically*): What have you been up to?

(*The noise increases in intensity. It is becoming unbearable*)

THE THIEF (*runs towards The Old Lady who is tied up to the chair and he shakes her*): What does this mean, old hag? What's this? Tell me, what's this?!

THE OLD LADY (*screams terrified*): Mr! Mr! I am scared, please! (*She bursts into tears*) Please!...

(*The Thief throws the wrapped up painting onto the table, he takes out his knife, and he remains in waiting. Sudden silence. He prudently steps towards the window. He looks out. The Old Lady cries softly*)

159

THE THIEF: Stop it! Stop it because it is not the police. It is an old ambulance.

THE OLD LADY: I am very afraid!

THE THIEF: If it is the police, you must be very afraid. Now, shut up!

(*A short pause when voices and various noises are heard. The Thief is watching the street*)

THE OLD LADY: Would you be so kind and leave? (*A pause*) Make sure you do not forget the painting! (*A pause*) Oh Lord, what a nightmare, and how afraid I am! (*A pause*) Why don't you do something, to calm me down? Why don't you leave immediately?!

THE THIEF: Who has asked you to answer the phone at night? (*A long pause. The Old Lady sits motionless. At last, The Thief lights a cigarette; he inhales passionately*)

THE OLD LADY: You should not smoke there. You could be seen from the street.

THE THIEF (*hides his cigarette. Slightly distracted*): OK... I understand. (*He smokes in his hand*) They don't seem to leave!... (…) And they gather like at the fair. In their slippers, in their dressing gowns, with their nightcaps... they gesticulate and they talk... They talk, damn it, and I am boiling!

THE OLD LADY: Aurica is giving birth.

THE THIEF: And why don't they take her to the maternity hospital, damn it?

THE OLD LADY: Mondan wishes the boy to be born at home. It's for the eighth time: each time it happened the same. Only that his wife gave birth to girls only.

THE THIEF (*bursts out laughing*): My word! (…) Do you want to smoke?

THE OLD LADY: No thank you. With coffee only.

160

THE THIEF: I don't have any coffee!

THE OLD LADY: It's in the cafetière, inside the chest of drawers. Open the large door on the left! I filled it in the evening: I am in the habit of leaving the coffee overnight to macerate. Then I put it in. It's delicious!

THE THIEF: I cannot leave until that bloke ends his fun!

THE OLD LADY: Please help yourself. It's my pleasure.

THE THIEF: Here?

THE OLD LADY: Yes. The cups are over there.

(*The Thief takes the cafetière and the cups out - the bulb in the street lights the stage*)

THE THIEF (*plugs the cafetière. He laughs*): That wants to say we've got a... rendez-vous!... (*He laughs again. A short pause*) So many things can happen to a person! Are your arms aching?

THE OLD LADY: No, I am fine.

THE THIEF: I'll untie you as soon as I finish making the coffee (*Harsh*) Be patient!

THE OLD LADY: I have not said a word!

THE THIEF: Damn you said! (*He turns towards her gesticulating*) You're manipulating the words: you're twisting them like this!... You believe yourself clever: 'I am feeling fine!'... Speak clearly! Spit it out! That's why I'm feeling like this in your presence. I believe you're trying to offend me.

THE OLD LADY: Mr, I am very tired.

THE THIEF: Ho, Ho, I've finished! (...) This coffee of yours will make you feel fourteen years old! (*Aside*) I'm not getting anywhere with this one. (*He fills in the cups, he places them on the table, and he unties her*) You can flap your wings now. But... You mustn't move from the branch!

THE OLD LADY (*rubs her arms and she stands a bit*)

161

THE OLD LADY (*grips the chair from underneath and she moves it closer to the table*)

THE THIEF: This is something else. (*He drinks*) Can you see? I made it strong.

THE OLD LADY: There is another exit. If you wish, I can show it to you!

THE THIEF: So that the guard from the nearby warehouse becomes famous.

THE OLD LADY: ...?

THE THIEF: First, I've studied the plan of the house! The photographs... I know everything: the neighbours, the entry doors, and the place where each painting hangs...!

THE OLD LADY: In this case, you can stay longer, can't you?

THE THIEF: Be glad! (*He sips from his coffee and he lits a cigarette*) Now, do you want a Kent cigarette?

THE OLD LADY: If you offer me one...

THE THIEF: When I have, I am not 'stingy'. Have it!

THE OLD LADY: What aren't you?

THE THIEF: (...) Somehow poor with the language! 'Stingy' means 'selfish' and 'miser' all in one. A kind of 'mean' - as you might say... Take it, because you are allowed! And don't call me kind again or something alike, because I'll get annoyed.

THE OLD LADY: I got into the habit saying 'thank you'... I learnt to be grateful.

THE THIEF (*helping himself*): Imagine you've done it. You are crossing my nerves with your polite ways! I suspect you're hiding something... You'll drown me as you drown a dog. And you might apologize... because you might cause... (*He imitates*) 'a slight pain in the neck!' (*Rough*) Damn it! (*He walks to the window and he looks out at the street. After a minute.*) That lot doesn't even think for a second that, tomorrow morning, they must go to work refreshed.

THE OLD LADY: If I could switch on the light, I could sip from the coffee.

THE THIEF: What are you on about now?!

THE OLD LADY: I do not spoil anything. (…) My neighbours are used to see the light on in here every night: around two o'clock!... If Mr Anton does not see the light on, he sounds the alarm: I am very old…

THE THIEF: I noticed it.

THE OLD LADY: They could believe that something has happened to me.

THE THIEF: Don't make things up! (…) If you're so eager, why not light a candle.

THE OLD LADY (*convincingly*): I am telling you the truth. It is for your good too: Mr Anton is a night watchman at the warehouse at the back of this house (…). Some time ago, I heard that some of his superiors had found him asleep in his booth: since then, every night, at two o'clock, I offer him a cup of coffee. I am expecting him now! We talk for about five minutes. (Stunned, *the Thief looks at her.*) He has got one year left until retirement, and he is alone… The coffee keeps him awake. I do not have coffee with him, because this would mean to open a topic of discussion and Mr. Anton hasn't got the time, what he does there is very important!... In exchange, this means a lot to me. The presence of a person stops time in its track.

THE THIEF: Providing I don't stop it for you for good! (*He shouts*) If you don't stop…! Doesn't he have anything better to do but to keep you awake? Why should he come back here?

THE OLD LADY: To drink his coffee.

THE THIEF (*idem*): And if the controller comes after him? If they find he has left his post?

THE OLD LADY: That is exactly what I want to tell you: that I am worried! I had plenty to think of until tonight.

This... unpleasant... obsession... (*She points upwards*) isn't showing yet. But I can easily forget! Do you know how strange it is to be anxious about something that could happen to a friend? You feel you are alive! You feel you are useful...

THE THIEF (*overwhelmed*): Wretched witch!

THE OLD LADY: Could I switch on the light?

THE THIEF: Don't move from there! (*He moves towards the switch*) If anything happens, you know what's going to happen.

THE OLD LADY: Just so that it does not happen, let it be light!

THE THIEF (*switches the light on and walks pointing his finger towards her*): After I leave from here, I'll go to church and I'll light a candle because I've escaped from you. Then, I'll get drunk!

THE OLD LADY (*sipping from her coffee*): When Mr Anton gets here, you will explain to him that you are a nephew of mine, and that I... am asleep.

THE THIEF: Well, well! Do you take me for an imbecile! (...) You'll tell him: That you are in your nightie, that you've run out of coffee, and that... he should go to the devil! (...) Do you have anything else to say?

THE OLD LADY: My heart is bothering me... Let's not quarrel!...

THE THIEF: It means that you have some reasoning left!

(*A short pause*)

THE OLD LADY: The candle has died out: will you strike the lighter once again? (*The Thief strikes it. The Old Lady blows into the flame*)

THE THIEF: What's got into you? (*He strikes it again*)

THE OLD LADY: That's it! For one moment, I had the sensation that we met before. It was only a thought. (...)

The same gesture towards the face, the same sudden touch, and you strike... Exactly the same movements... The same look...

THE THIEF: Do you really need to light?

THE OLD LADY: Thank you! (...) I always disliked the way he lit his cigarette... Actually, even since then I presumed that he was a misanthrope. However, when my husband was gaoled, he would send provisions to me! (*She laughs softly*) He was courting me roughly like an anxious man: after each lot of three parcels, he would call me into his office and utter the same words to me. I imagine he considered it very lascivious that is why he had never changed it or, he considered it to be the right formula for well-planned tactics. He would offer me a cigarette, he... (*She reproduces The Thief's gesture of striking the lighter*) and he would say: 'We haven't got the time, because problems are gulping us'. But, tonight' by eight o'clock, you'll go to Hotel Park to the receptionist and you'll tell him 'the carnation doesn't smell, but it's still a flower'. The answer will be: 'Please, be welcomed'...If he doesn't reply 'Please, be welcomed', you don't enter.

(*She laughs*)

THE THIEF (*bursts into laughter*)

THE OLD LADY (*continues, with obvious pleasure*): 'You'll wait for me, because I wish to tell you something heart to heart, which will interest you'. He would wink! Good bye!... I would turn up here and I would wait for the parcels. Of course, I never responded to his 'orders'.

(*The Thief goes to the window. He looks out*)

165

THE OLD LADY: He was vulgar. He was brutal... He would smell of wet clothes, kept for too long in an enclosed space... And, I do not understand why, although he maintained he wanted to help us, I always had the sensation that the initiative of the painter's arrest was his.

THE THIEF: As you are going on, you want to believe that you were the only one to be right! I wish to inform you that the topic bothers me. (*Bluntly*) Better come clean about the reason why he was gaoled!

THE OLD LADY: He informed a minister that library books kept being burnt in the name of the people: that the local arts councillors were incompetent!... He was uttering the truth. But, as you well know, love of truth and fanaticism cannot go hand in hand. He did not have a chance.

THE THIEF: The truth - on his side, fanaticism - on the others' side! Why not the reverse?

THE OLD LADY: Because nearly everything can be seen now! Time has passed. Time tidies up values. Some climb on its back and scream... They cover it in words. Time shakes them off, like an elephant shakes aunts off, and it goes on and on! The wooden fence and the adobe wall remain the same. Only a real wall made by an honest man remains standing! The wall can be anything: a painting, a book, a theatre part, an invention, a utilitarian building, ...and music...

THE THIEF: Because of Nicu Arin, some people got into trouble! (...) Perhaps you did not wish revenge, but that's the result. However, I don't wish to cause you too much damage for what you did, you did it out of love... Anyway, you are somebody. I want to tell you're a daredevil, that you are wicked - as a friend of mine says - but I don't know anything else about you. (*He raises his voice*) And I don't even want to know! (*He shouts*) Are

166

you OK? (…) And don't try to trick me any more because you won't succeed! I've listened to you long enough; don't even bother! Do you understand? It hasn't worked! Besides… look at the entire nuisance caused by those people in the street… because they are not minding their own business. (*He screams*) And if I told you are somebody, I told you so that you are content and damn shut up now! (*He breathes heavily; his agitated eyes look out of their sockets. Silence. He walks into the room, he stops behind the curtains, he is terribly nervous. He notices the clock on the chest of drawers, he holds it in his hand like a mace*) What's this?

THE OLD LADY: Can I reply?

THE THIEF: I've asked you.

THE OLD LADY: A present.

THE THIEF (*is calm*): It doesn't work.

THE OLD LADY: It stopped when the painter died.

THE THIEF (*handles it as a weapon*): It's perfect for hitting someone on the head. Have you thought of it?

THE OLD LADY: I do not have the time.

THE THIEF (*bursts into laughter. Softened by so much fun, he lets himself down into a chair. He is pointing to her with his finger, choking*): You Thief… you Thief, I wasn't wrong! I wasn't wrong at all: Believe me… ha, ha, ha… I respect… Hear me: 'I haven't got the time!' Ha, ha, ha!

(*The Old Lady watches him in silence. Suddenly he laughs embarrassingly under her gaze; another kind of laughter*)

THE THIEF: Ha, ha, ha! (*A short pause*) You don't even hate me. (*Pause*) One feels sick… But there's nothing, look: I'll overlook your disgust - as a gentleman I'm - and… I'll re… pair… your… object! (*The Old Lady is*

167

startled) What about this? (…) It means something that it stopped then. Now it will start again! It will sound its tick-tock, tick-tock…! I can also be mean, can't I? Tick-tock, tick-tock…

THE OLD LADY: Since His death, all timepieces stopped in this house!

THE THIEF: Excellent! Here, the timepieces… have waited for… their maker! Here Time… will be measured from the moment of my arrival onwards! A new age has begun: the destruction age! If we haven't learnt to measure happiness in units of time, then suffering must have clear units of measurement: like a year, a month, an hour, a second! Suffering has the time unit of a thousandth of a second and, after you have enjoyed so many opportunities, do you still believe that these seconds of suffering have exhausted you!

THE OLD LADY: I implore you to be careful: you are hitting me!

THE THIEF: You wished for it, and… enough! No: you must see, - if we must be so close -, all has been turned around: feel how everything has changed, how everything already aimed at becoming something has suddenly turned into something else!... "Has time stopped in its tracks?!...". Hear these fibs! You're afraid and you've made all sorts of arrangements. The arrangement with the guards, the arrangement with the clock… How old are you?

THE OLD LADY: Eighty-three.

THE THIEF: And why haven't you died yet?

THE OLD LADY: I have always been busy!

THE THIEF: I don't believe you! You're scared of this! You won't leave and you're making people dizzy in your frozen time. (*He sits down; he takes his screwdriver out, some needles, etc.*) From the distance we'll arrange a small operation: so that you can feel your departure; to

168

the devil: and you'll find out, how, when... you can go, if the wonders of artistic garbage that people create are worth anything! (*He shows her his knife*) I'm telling you not to try anything! (*He starts his work*)

THE OLD LADY (*who is obviously fighting with herself*): Are you a clockmaker?

THE THIEF: No, but I got damned links with time! Once when I was born though I shouldn't have been - so that you can understand me, - my apologies: I've landed in the wrong epoch! Then, this wicked *Nothing Can Be Done* robs me with promises: it gets me into all sorts of trouble, which seem clear to me, and then, the boys in blue arrest me! According to their custom, they hide me and... My time stops in its tracks. This is my personal opinion: a few days ago, I started going out again, and this morning, when I was having a wash, I saw in the mirror that the hairs inside my nostrils have already gone grey! Well?

THE OLD LADY (*ironically*): I do not understand you! You are much too profound...!

THE THIEF: I wouldn't say so, on the contrary...!

THE OLD LADY: But, because you 'work' with... the knife, by the way, about the knife: when ours came to power, - the dreamers were overwhelmed by enthusiasm!... (*She is uttering nostalgically*) 'With the metal from the gaols/ we can overturn the exploiters...!'. (*She laughs softly*)

THE THIEF (*bursts out*): When this one begins to gnaw at time, you'll hear greater poems! Ha, ha, ha, have I scared you?... You know the text: Tick-tock, tick-tock I am quiet! I am as quiet as a mouse! Well... (*He is working*)

THE OLD LADY (*trying not to watch him*): When my husband was in gaol, there were round eyeholes in the wooden doors of the gaol covered in round tin covers. When someone wished to see what was going on inside the cell, he would move the tin cover away and he would watch. With one eye only! (…) My husband was terribly bothered by this interference in his intimate life, and one day… he drew on the eyehole… a knife pointed downwards! (*She is extremely tired: she is speaking slowly, with great effort. Unmoved, The Thief is working*) From that moment on, when an eye appeared in the eyehole… he imagined how the pointed end of the knife would penetrate the indiscreet pupil of the eye and he would laugh. Because of his cheerfulness, …of his permanent joy… they believed…

THE THIEF: …that he was mad!

THE OLD LADY: …that he was feeling fine and then he was discharged. What fun he made of it all!...

THE THIEF: And with good reason! The bloke was not stupid… (*He is working*)

THE OLD LADY (*slightly startled*): He had absorbed me…! A long time ago, when the world seemed… *to have been created only for me*, I entered Him by means of my beautiful body! – And I could not exit again. 'I was the straw he hanged on desperately when circumstances attempted to engulf him. I was the Artist: I represented All the artists in the world when I defended what was unique in Him. And the saviour… I took away the hand from his forehead and I did not move: the perfect… stretched body of the painter… it was… an immense… sign… of warning… on the immaculate white sheet…". (*She falls asleep. She snores like a child*)

(*The Thief places the watch next to him. He is holding his chin in his clasped hands, he watches her; he is muddled up. He stands up. He scrutinizes the room. He walks to the chest of drawers, he takes out a wrap, he places it over her shoulders, and he remains like that for a while. The Old Lady sighs in her sleep. Strangely, she feels protected*)

Curtain

Half an hour later.

Before the curtain is up, soft music is born out of the darkness by the short sighs of a violin. The same scenery. Quiet and focussed on his work, The Thief is sitting at the table repairing the clock. The music becomes louder, generating a feeling of insecurity; it will extend into a symphony of dynamic rhythms, as if musical phrases are read from back to front. When the melody reaches paroxysm, it is suddenly interrupted...a moment of quietness, then the noise of the street can be heard. In addition, there is the noise made by the party from over the road. A domestic atmosphere is created on the stage. The Old Lady is snoring softly.

THE THIEF *(working)*: Damn it, how precious do you believe yourself to be! If you associate yourself to things that appear eternal to you, you can pour a bucket of superiority over your head on this very spot: so nobody can reach you (…) 'I was the straw he desperately hanged on when circumstances attempted to engulf him. I was the Artist: I represented All the artists in the world…!'. Rubbish! Empty words. And you consider yourself to have the right to be happy too. Well, you're not! Because, until the end, you remain a poor being that's mixed up - I still don't understand the reason - with an object that you think immortal. I… I mean to hold only on what must die, and I am happy. I'm even more content because while living I've been learning. I learnt to be happy in my childhood. Recently only I

171

came to understand how great it is to enjoy good health and a young body... I remember how happy I was just at the blink of an eye. I doubt that I'll ever be as happy as this again! That's why I insist, without hesitation, that this heaven exists only in my memory. The hell ...is here. Now!... Living as long as possible, I insure myself for a greater part of past heaven - and a smaller and smaller one of hell, here and... before! (…) You're asleep... What do you care? You've almost escaped. (…) I'd like to wake you up to ask you a question, which might clarify everything entirely, but what's the point? I've come upon two words that no one has ever been able to make me understand: the word 'fight' and the word 'guilty'. The first word is the most absurd one because it always presupposes the existence of a victorious individual against a defeated one - therefore peace can never exist. The second word puzzles me. Guilty: 'who'and vis-à-vis 'whom'? (…) The only guilty individual, the guiltiest of them all is the Lord! For being unable to suffer his solitude with dignity, he created man, so that someone could judge him! When you are accounted, you have the proof that you are not alone... Since then all our actions have been directed towards judging him: good deeds reject his primitive judgement. Guilty individuals aren't guilty, but the judge who divides them! (…)

(*All quiet. The clock begins to sound suddenly. Surprised, in his pure and simple fear, The Thief throws it upwards. He tries to catch it in the now amplified racket of the ringing phone. The Old Lady wakes up*)

THE OLD LADY: Good morning!... (*She lifts the receiver*) Yes, Anton, it's me... I... (*She realizes the phone is out of order*) But, the telephone is out of order!... I have not even got a dialling tone. Not even a dialling tone... What are you doing? Why are you still here?

THE THIEF: (*standing, he is trembling, he is ready to kick the clock on the floor. He changes his mind. He stoops, he lifts it and, he puts it on the table laughing*) It's working! I've succeeded in the end.

THE OLD LADY: I am sorry!

(*The Thief walks to the window, he lifts one corner of the netting, and he puffs air. He suddenly tenses himself, he presses his stomach with one hand, and he bends. He sighs*)

THE OLD LADY: You are not too well with your nerves.

THE THIEF: How long has this coffee been in that rusty box for?

THE OLD LADY: It was fresh! I put it there last night.

THE THIEF (*imitates her*): 'I put it there last night...'! Perhaps, a month ago!

THE OLD LADY: I believe that it is emotions more likely! When I was at the front...

THE THIEF (*groans, he goes and sits on a chair*): Don't tell me you were in the artillery... that I'll damn give all up, and I'll jump outside right into that ambulance, which is waiting for all the idiots of the district to show off!

THE OLD LADY (*candid*): You see; only the strongest young men, the technically skilled ones were fighting at tanks...!

THE THIEF: Had you studied some illustrated magazines for about a week, they... might have recruited you too!

THE OLD LADY (*idem*): I believe that Colonel Boghiu would have been displeased: he liked my hands very much, and at tanks... they work with Vaseline! You

173

know, he often used to tell me, that I do not really know what an extraordinary woman I am…!

THE THIEF: He should have asked me, I would have given you… references…!

THE OLD LADY: He would kiss my hand here, at the beginning of the palm, where I had a little vein, which was bifurcating into a blue colour…

THE THIEF (*stretches in pain evaluating her in his gaze*): Poor him… gullible man…!

THE OLD LADY (*agreeing*): Yes, he was very much in love…! But… what was I saying?

THE THIEF (*groaning*): How was that old man serenading you?

THE OLD LADY: You are wrong: he wasn't old at all!... He was very able. He was the youngest colonel!

THE THIEF: I heard that it wasn't difficult: as the Russians were hacking them at the front line, there was a fast promotion through the ranks.

THE OLD LADY: He proved himself in Ardeal, in spite of the others. He had a bag full of shining medals!... When he found that I landed in his patch with a military order in hand, he sent me directly to the field hospital… (…) After an hour… he wasn't any more. At Oarba de Mureş!

THE THIEF: I know. I collected snowdrops there. I caught butterflies too!

(*A short pause.*)

THE OLD LADY: Why aren't you going to the toilet? Due to the emotions you are going through, it's perfectly understandable…

THE THIEF: From the way those swollen eyes of yours are shining, you must be plotting again!

THE OLD LADY: Excuse me, but according to the manner in which you are speaking to me, you are only showing a childish endeavour to suppress fear. Aren't you afraid that you might be despised... exactly for this?

THE THIEF (*having only one concern now*): It could be (...) I'm going to the loo, but stay put! Don't muddle me, because I haven't anything against you. Do you understand me? (*He goes to the toilet.*) Don't move from there, otherwise... I'll have to deal with you! (*From inside the toilet*) Speak to me now. So that I can hear you!

THE OLD LADY: I could say you are my guest! I could take you into the street and everybody could see how we say good-bye!

THE THIEF: Oi! Only a number of police officers are missing from amongst those nosy parkers outside!

THE OLD LADY: This always happens!... You tell a man not to cross a footbridge when he comes back from the pub, but he is convinced that he does not need any advice. (*She stands up; she takes the large candle, which she had first carried onto the stage. She goes round the table*) One day, he will fall into the abyss. He will break something! If you remind him that you had warned him, he could kill you: his drunkenness has passed. It is irrelevant to him. I want to point out: the drunkenness! What is important now is that he is shown some compassion! He must be helped. So that he could feel like... 'an invalid'!

THE THIEF (*from the wings*): I've always been keen on infant school lessons!

THE OLD LADY (*has reached the space left empty by the removing of the painting. She stares intensely at the device that 'should' function*): All of them act like this. People behave like this, because their education requires only their adaptation to 'a' society, and not the understanding that they 'live only once'! Man is exceptionally evil: animals feed only on the individuals from other species, while man…!

THE THIEF (*comes out*): Oi! What are you doing there?

THE OLD LADY (*startled. She hits the wall with the candle, as high as she can, trying to reach the alarm device. She does not reach it*)

THE THIEF (*takes the knife out, He prepares to throw it*): What are you trying to do? (*He sees that The Old Lady cannot reach the device. He advances calmly, and he puts the knife back. The Old Lady steps back, she prepares to throw the object, which she is holding. She is checking her pocket; she takes out a box of matches. For the first time, The Old Lady changes the way of addressing*)

THE OLD LADY: What do you want?

THE THIEF: A candle can't be lit with a lighter. (*He strikes a match*) Please do not tremble: I can't light it. (…) Thank you! (*He accompanies her by the arm.*)

THE OLD LADY: Good, But I have only tried to stop you.

THE THIEF (*calm, decisive*): I've seen it. I respect you for this, but enough is enough! I must get rid of you.

THE OLD LADY: The manner in which you are talking to me now scares me: Why don't you address me informally any more?

THE THIEF: I respect the dead, Madam. (*He is almost holding her gently by the arm*)

THE OLD LADY: I have asked you to control yourself. Your nerves are on the edge!

THE THIEF: It is the first wise thing uttered by you. You must know I'm going to finish you quickly… But I don't want it to happen here. (*He is pointing to the window*) I must stay a bit longer, until those dummies disperse and your body… could hinder me. Let's step into the other room. (…) Please!

THE OLD LADY (*tears herself away*): Are you mad! Oh Lord...! (*Places the table between them*) They will condemn you to death!

THE THIEF: I beg you not to be afraid, it's nothing!... At the beginning it's a bit uncomfortable, a bit painful, but afterwards... it's great! You begin to dream. You sink into a velvety warm liquid... at a certain moment you don't even need air! Someone who was smothered with a pillow and who escaped with his life told me about it: you begin to remember all sorts of extraordinary things. You'll even like it, I promise you! On my word of honour, you deserve that someone compromises oneself in order to render you such a service! I implore you, why are you trembling? I don't like people who tremble. I don't like it at all, because it gives me the sensation that I am performing an operation, which harms you, and I only want to make myself useful to you. Don't you feel that all I wish is to make myself useful to you? (...) Why can't we get on well together?

THE OLD LADY (*out of breath*): Anton will come and if I don't answer, he will certainly think that something has happened to me! He will ring the police station, the director, the chief of section, Mrs Viorica and he will alert the entire neighbourhood...!

THE THIEF (*shouts, he bangs the floor with his foot*): Can you see how you're trying... to distract me once again?

THE OLD LADY: They will catch you! Be careful: concentrate! Try to concentrate: they'll catch you!... They will punish you terribly!... Be calm! Calm down! Breathe in deeply. Come on, breathe in, and concentrate... Breathe in! Like this!... Be calm... Think carefully: If something happens to me, they will surely catch you and... (*Exhausted, she lets herself down into a chair*) they will condemn you to death... (*She is crying*)

177

THE THIEF (*confused*): I've asked you not to cry!... I'm asking you, and... you... (*Abruptly*) Damn you with the manners of a mongrel, shut up! Shut up, damn you, I forgive you!

THE OLD LADY (*is crying*)

THE THIEF: I forgive you if you promise me that, when that individual turns up, you'll send him away!

THE OLD LADY: I promise...

THE THIEF: Then, remain here. Upon your word of honour that you won't trick me!

THE OLD LADY: Believe me. Upon my word of honour...

(*A short pause*)

THE THIEF (*content*): I see: not bad. For the time being! (*He sits down. Relaxed*) It's rather late, but if I were to apply myself seriously, I could get something out of you! (*He laughs*) What do you think? (*The Old Lady takes a sip from the coffee cup*) You're feeling better. It's passed! Do you fancy a cigarette?

THE OLD LADY: I hate you! Because you feel sorry for me. You, who would drag me by my feet...

A VOICE (*from outside*): Mrs Alice!

THE OLD LADY: Nothing can be more distressing...

THE THIEF (*horror-stricken*): He's here!

THE OLD LADY:...nothing can be more lamentable than a woman who was once beautiful!

THE THIEF: Is your name Alice?

THE OLD LADY: Yes.

THE THIEF: Can't you hear that he's here?

THE OLD LADY: I've been waiting for him.

THE THIEF: What are you going to do?

A VOICE: Mrs Alice!

THE OLD LADY: I have not decided yet!

THE THIEF: But you've promised me!?

THE OLD LADY: Because you have been menacing me!

THE THIEF: You've tricked me! Do not make a move: I must think... Stay still!

THE OLD LADY: Count me out, please; fear disgusts me.
(*She walks towards the window*)

THE THIEF: Come back when I tell you!

THE OLD LADY: Don't be stupid, please!... (*She opens the window*) Good evening, Mr Anton!

A VOICE: Good evening, Mrs Alice, the weather's wonderful tonight.

THE OLD LADY: I have been feeling it for so long and I still enjoy it. Do you want to come in?

THE THIEF (*breaks the clock from the corner of the table. He picks it up to throw it in the direction of The Old Lady, who turns towards him*) I've... I've... stopped him. (*Hopeful*) Wasn't this what you wanted?

A VOICE: Has something happened, Mrs Alice?

THE OLD LADY: No. The clock fell from above the chest of drawers. Aren't you coming in?

A VOICE: Thank you, Mrs Alice, but I've got company. There's no danger for me to fall asleep: We're waiting for Aurica to give birth.

THE OLD LADY: I see. All the neighbours have gathered.

A VOICE: Mondan has brought the demijohn onto the steps and he's waiting... with about twenty empty glasses nearby. If she gives birth to a son, he'll invite us all for a drink, if not...!

THE OLD LADY (*laughs quietly, pleased*): I do not wish it onto him, but...

THE THIEF: Send him away, damn it!

A VOICE: Ha, ha, ha! It would be the eighth broken demijohn! Ha, ha, ha!...

THE OLD LADY: A moment only, Mr Anton! (*She turns her back to the curtains she is holding tight with her hand*) Mr! But your look is confused!... And your face

179

devastated!? (…) Someone wrote that the more we experience fear, the more sensuality we show... (…) My compliments!... From this point of view, you are a man… as one has rarely seen!

THE THIEF (*out of breath*): I'll kill you! I'll make mincemeat of you… I'll tear this rubbish for which you keep boiling me!

THE OLD LADY: I shall turn my back so that you can have more courage. (*She is addressing the person outside*.) Excuse me, Mr Anton, but I had to check if the coffee is ready. I was plugging the cafetière when the telephone rang.

A VOICE: That's why I came: because of the telephone! You didn't answer.

THE OLD LADY: It is out of order.

A VOICE: I don't think there is an awful lot wrong with it.

THE THIEF (*behind The Old Lady*): If you're going to open the door, then, I'll fill the house with corpses!

THE OLD LADY: One moment, Mr Anton! (*She turns*) You look paler, Mr. Perhaps… you are covered in a cold sweat. Your breath is heavy and violent palpitations madden you underneath the stern… A feeling of dread, of panic that passes through your feet turns on you… and drags you with it… (*She laughs like a queen*) With your hand tight on the knife, you can neither advance nor retrieve!

THE THIEF (*snorts, his hand piercing his own collar, which he is tearing*)

THE OLD LADY: You cannot kill me, because you'll be discovered immediately.

A VOICE: Mrs Alice!

THE OLD LADY: And you cannot destroy the painting either, because then I would renounce everything and I would scream!

THE THIEF: Mongrel! Mo….

THE OLD LADY: No! Do not shout! The window is open! (*Almost with compassion*) You're behaving like a child!!!...

A VOICE: Mrs Alice!

THE OLD LADY (*interrupts herself*): Tonight, I am very impolite, Mr Anton. Moreover, most of all distracted. I remember why I have not lifted the receiver; it happened because I was convinced that it was you. This time, I worked out that the bell was like a warning telling me that you will arrive.

A VOICE: I said I thank you, but…

THE OLD LADY: No worries, Mr Anton. I am waiting for you tomorrow evening. Then I will have coffee with you. I will tell you something funny.

A VOICE: OK Madam, kiss your hands!

THE OLD LADY: Good bye, Mr Anton!... If it is a boy, ask Mr Mondan to offer you an extra glass to drink on my behalf.

A VOICE: Thank you, you're very kind.

THE OLD LADY (*apart*): Good-bye… (*She closes the window. She draws the curtains. Quiet*)

THE THIEF (*after a while*): What was this?

THE OLD LADY (*quietly, looks at him curiously. Then she laughs softly, as if to herself*): Nothing, my man… I remembered how I used to be. A long time ago…!

THE THIEF: You scared me: I thought you were not going to keep your word! (*He bursts out laughing*) Damn you, you scared me!... (*He unwinds laughing; a laughter to match the fright he has experienced - with groans, hiccups and short pauses*) But, you must not do it again. Don't try it again!... You're calling for it…

THE OLD LADY: This Saturday, I baked some pastry. Would you like some? (*She uncovers the tray covered with a tea towel, which is set on the chest of drawers. She* *carries it to the table*) I do not eat them. Mr Hoza likes them very much.

THE THIEF: What time will he turn up?

THE OLD LADY: You have misunderstood me. This is not a hotel!

THE THIEF: You get angry. unexpectedly... You should have put caraway or poppy seeds in it. Not both of them. They're too much of a mixture.

THE OLD LADY: I did not have enough of any of them. It is not easy to find them...

THE THIEF: They're good anyway.

THE OLD LADY: Mr Hoza likes them. (...) He comes here only on Sundays, at two o'clock in the afternoon: He tells me what has happened at the crossroads. What cars had collided, how badly drivers drive... (*The Thief chews and stares in the distance*) Mr Hoza cannot stand the owners of luxury cars in particular. He says that they are fast at showing off their bundles of money and at asking him to write his Report speedily... He does not give them a fine out of scorn and aversion. (*She watches The Thief who looks a bit surprised and who is continuously chewing, but without swallowing*) They moralize you in exchange. (...) Mr Horza is convinced that he writes his reports with difficulty because he stutters.

THE THIEF (*chews*): Ya!

(*The Old Lady goes silent. She stares at him. The Thief is chewing slowly, lost in thought. Suddenly, The Old Lady*)

THE OLD LADY: You do not like to listen to me.

THE THIEF: No... (*After a while*) When I do this, (*He points to his swollen cheek*) when I happen to chew something, nothing interests me any longer... I tried to convince someone of the advantages of this happening, but it didn't work out: she thought I was mad! (*With conviction*) It's the only thing that doesn't bother anyone else in this world: to chew like this, like a ruminant. More so, in comparison to others, you forget! I say, if you have something that takes long to chew one can forget everything! (…) Do you know what it means to take something out from your belt like a bit of bread, hidden there inside a cloth, and to begin to chew it?...To begin to chew it while you are looking at a brown long legged spider, which has come out from behind the bed standing next to the wall, and which is carefully climbing, step by step, over the texture of the plastering - which touches its belly, fast to start with, then slower and slower... Soft warmth touches you from the back to the groin, and you chew and chew…! It stops, stiff, in its legs: it turns small, very small, then it becomes bigger, it turns a pink colour and you get a fixed stare… and you chew… and chew… That moment in time you thank God you're alone. (*He breathes out with difficulty, because he experienced what he has just explained*) Or… can you imagine what it means to chew a crust of bread while you are beaten up? (…) What relief it can bring you, while others fret to give you a wet shirt!...

THE OLD LADY: It is a world I do not understand…

THE THIEF: I'm telling you all these things because, after you came back with the security guard - no one has succeeded! - you got my trust. I'll be dead if I don't like you. You've stirred something, here. Something I didn't know existed.

THE OLD LADY: You are far too young. You are hasty to conclude. Have you been more experienced, you might have seen or heard many more things…

THE THIEF: You mustn't think of me as being mad… Or that I've a pile of dung in my head, but I'd like you not to get angry if… if… (*He timidly stretches his hand*

183

towards The Old Lady's face) Don't be afraid, I mean no harm! (*With his fingers, he gets hold of her chin. He touches her face upwards and he caresses her head*) Your flesh is soft and your temples are sweaty... Your head is small: fragile, like a girl's, you've hemp-seed coloured hair, (...) If you behave yourself, I'll take care of you! You must only be quiet and you'll have nothing to lose. Besides, you're alone and suffering. I shall visit you often: you fix me a time and it's done. Nobody needs to know! (*He caresses her head and her face*)

THE OLD LADY (*retrieves slightly*): See if these are better. Mr Hoza prefers the well roasted ones!

THE THIEF: He, he, he, mad woman!... You've got under my skin!?

THE OLD LADY: Help yourself. I noticed you calm down when you eat something!

THE THIEF (*sits down and helps himself*): I believe I should say, 'Thanks'!

THE OLD LADY: We seem to understand one another. (*She is humming, a tune. Surprised, The Thief is looking at her*) I cannot remember the lyrics! (*She is singing*) 'The wheels of the mill go,/ Tzac, tzac, tzac./ The miller's wife... la, la, la, la./ tzac, tzac, ...'. Do you know it?

THE THIEF (*confused*): No, what has come onto you?

THE OLD LADY: I cannot remember but (*She sings*) 'The miller's wife is at the spinning wheel, tzac, tzac, tzac,/ And the miller is longing for her, tzac, tzac, tzac...'. I've forgotten it. Before I used to sing this a lot! At all the parties! (*She is singing*) La, la, la, la, la, la, la, la,/ tzac, tzac, tzac./ La, la, la, la, la, la, la, la/ tzac/ tzac/ tzac.

(*The Thief is carried away and starts singing: he knows the words. They sing together. They are having fun; it is moving and tragic at the same time. They feel it 'differentl'" and they embark on having fun almost in despair. When they finish singing, the silence, which none of them wants, is settling in. The Old Lady's breathing is affected by the effort. He is quiet. Suddenly, The Old Lady leans over The Thief)*

THE OLD LADY: Come closer (…) Good! Now, look at me! At my eyes! Deeply! Can you observe that watery grey circle round the cornea? (*They are getting their heads even closer together*) The circle named 'arcus senilis'! This is a certain sign of senility!

THE THIEF (*takes a close look at her eyes, then at her entire face and he utters abruptly*): Your husband was a disgusting man. And you were a disgusting woman for letting yourself be painted naked. (*He points to the nudes on the walls*) Everything about you is disgusting: you're full of airs and graces; you're making wry faces like a monkey…! Even when you mount one another you don't say what you're up to like ordinary people: you say you're making love… Sheep don't tug, the cockerel doesn't step over the hen, dogs aren't in heat, and horses don't mount: they make love. What do you know about love?

THE OLD LADY (*pushes the tray towards him*): Try some more…

THE THIEF: Do you want me to smash them onto your head? Now *you* imagine that I'm obsessed with chewing…!

THE OLD LADY: It took me half a day to bake them… I thought you might like them.

THE THIEF (*looks at her suspiciously. At last, he decides to do her 'a favour'*): Which ones would you say are the best? (…) These? (*He helps himself*)

THE OLD LADY: It depends how you like them…

185

THE THIEF (*he munches from a stick. Then*): Life… It's not worth the effort to abandon it. Only out of kindness, one feels like giving a hand to those who don't know how to mock at her and help her crack… That's enough! Fortune, poverty; gonorrhoea, health; honesty, shame; potency, impotence; despair, indifference. Treason… belief… loneliness… liberty… knowledge… art aren't worth any money! (…) Perhaps love. Until you learn what love is! Otherwise, it's a smelly air, which disintegrates with the first breeze… And you're telling me how to make salty sticks!

(A short pause)

THE OLD LADY: Have you ever opened… your chest?

THE THIEF: You mean, I should spit it all out.

THE OLD LADY: If you feel like it. You sound quite troubled: though I cannot say I am particularly interested.

THE THIEF: What on earth could still interest you now, when… (*Pointing to her throat*) crack!... Finished! Perhaps how it might be beyond there! Anyway, I guarantee you: it's better than here. Because, can you see what's happening here? Do you know? (…) Amazing punishment for my shaken soul!...(…) You know how important it's when you love for the first time: you've been in love! Don't deny it: all your torment has its reason at last… (*He slowly transgresses all his intuitions about THE OLD LADY into his emotional territory*) A long time ago, a man's heart had throbbed when he could see your knee, when he could hear your step, when you would run amongst the willows to have a dip into the river and when, feeling weak in his legs, he would let himself down on a stone and would stare like that at the sun… His eyes would ache if he were to keep them open to let the sun burn the reflexion of your white body in them, while the image of your body was slowly floating on the waters passing under his stone... (*He comes back*) You've also been very important! (*Again, as above*) Especially... When you were caressing your child, the stranger was resting his back against the fence. He closed his eyes and suddenly, the wind, which was uncoiling your child's hair in your fingers, and your voice, which was making him dizzy, talked to him. Moreover, the smell of your shirt reached him and he breathed in the aroma of your armpits.

THE OLD LADY (*surprisingly opaque*): I... could not have children!

THE THIEF (*excited*): I'm not talking about you! (...) I was talking about someone who was in love with my brother's wife. Who stole the money she was accounting, so that she - who was innocent - would be sent to gaol. Who had advised his brother to admit to being 'guilty' so that she could bring up his son! Who imagined that when his brother had replaced his wife Maria in gaol, happiness might touch him...! Who, after a month only, had to bury Maria, the love of his life for whom he had committed all these sins, because... She had died. Of cancer! I organised her burial with fifteen priests, with two choirs and a brass band. I took her in a van followed by fifteen taxies: I walked to the grave with the child in my arms... (...) The child is being brought up by an old woman who is so unable that the only thing she can do for him is: cry and cry!... I haven't got any money. Do you understand? (*Worked up*) That's why I'm here muzzle to muzzle with you: in order to rob you! I'm proud! (*He screams*) I'm proud I'm a Thief! I'm proud I steal! Call me 'Thief'. Call me 'Thief' or are you deaf?!

THE OLD LADY: Mr... M'... Thief?!

THE THIEF: Call me 'Thief', f... you artist! Call me!

THE OLD LADY (*desperate*): Thief!

THE THIEF (*smirking*): Try to utter it without 'Mr'? Say it again!

THE OLD LADY (*calls*): Assassin! You are a caddish Thief, a murderer of the lowest kind! You are a dirty Thief! A poisonous worm!

THE THIEF (*surprised, but somehow calm against the avalanche of epithets*): Your tongue is running free! You're close. But the matter with: of the lowest kind, must be replaced with cad, rude, churl, boorish swine!... Otherwise, you've managed to avoid the courtesy that was crossing my nerves.

THE OLD LADY (*candidly*): Did it feel good?

THE THIEF: He! You're damn right!...

THE OLD LADY: Thank you... When you like some more, you must only ask. First, you must seriously scare me; otherwise, I cannot do it!

THE THIEF (*roars with laughter, chocking, hiccupping in surprise*): A she-devil, damn you... Ha, ha, ha, as mad as a hatter!... You're somebody, you convinced me!

THE OLD LADY: I dare speak to you like this, because... in a way, ...we are alike! (...) I have also been stealing! For about two years now! I do not know how it all started, but it suddenly dawned on me like this. Then I liked it!

THE THIEF: Listen: leave them, because I smoked them! I also snubbed a clerk who, having lost some documents and, in order to get on well with the life-prisoners in gaol, was stressing that... he had been condemned for murder!...

THE OLD LADY (*after a while*): The procedure sickens me, but he should not have lied... No. I was talking to you about my latest passion. I have... a reason: I donated to the state paintings and a house of a value in excess of two millions! I must recuperate part of it at least, mustn't I? (...) However... Let me show you the collection!

188

(*With difficulty, she takes out a wrap from under the chest of drawers in which there are some wrapped objects*) Will you put this parcel on the chair?

THE THIEF (*does it*): Have you got money?... Gold... Jewellery?... (*He shakes the wrap*) Some old art objects?

THE OLD LADY: I am not so up-to-date... I am only a beginner. Put them there. Good. (*He unfolds the wrap*) Look!

THE THIEF: Are you mocking at me?

THE OLD LADY (*She is showing her loot with the most bewildering candour*): On the left, it's a universal key. I stole it from Ifrim. He still owns me ten lei! From the money I lent him to buy a bottle of wine: he is a very bad debtor... I wanted to be sure (...) Here, in this paper parcel, there is a very precious object!... Ermine visited me when the museum was being repaired this winter. When she left, she stealthily put my gold earrings into her handbag! I saw it! (*Victorious*): Well, here you can find the clip in bone imitation brought from Poland by her lover!... I outwitted her! What do you say to that!

THE THIEF: Ducky, you're mad.

THE OLD LADY: Just a moment! What do you think might be hidden amongst these blue cartons!... Well? A congratulations card! I sent it to a painter who did not deserve the words written on it! I watched the postman at her gate all day long: in order to solve my problem! When I heard him deliver the mail, I was about to fall asleep on the bench. I let him go, then I went to the impostor's landlady and I tricked her and told her that I was delivering a precious gift to her tenant: I had a lovely big dog in my arms...! Made of velvet. I left it on the table, and while the landlady was marvelling at how expensive and beautiful that toy was, I stealthily subtracted the card! This one!

THE THIEF: I had enough. Don't you have something else?

THE OLD LADY: This is the cane...

THE THIEF: I asked you to spare me! (*He walks towards the window*) I'm going to change the scenery.

THE OLD LADY: This is Artur Iovan's cane!

THE THIEF (*is stunned; he turns abruptly*): Do you want to say that...?

THE OLD LADY: It is his cane!

THE THIEF: Is this all?

THE OLD LADY: That... I wanted to tell you how I stole it!

THE THIEF: Are you sure, you didn't wish to say something else?

THE OLD LADY: What else could I say? I have already told you about Artur Iovan: He was the one who would invite me to Park Hotel... He would search his wallet with trembling hands. One night, when he leaned his cane against the fence, ... I took it and I ran as fast as I could! For quite a long time, I could hear him shout 'Catch The Thief! Catch The Thief!...'. He could not move without his cane! (...) When my husband came back from gaol, he went to his house to thank him... for the way in which he had taken care of me. - Of course, I did not tell him anything! - Then, Artur Iovan slapped him; he insulted him and called him 'court licker'! You are here in the name of one like him...!

THE THIEF: I know he's dirt, but I need the money! Do you understand?... I'll take the money and... the end! Forever! (...) The only thing I can promise you is that I'm stealing the painting for whatever it might fetch, and I'll bring it back! After a while, even if you weren't... here...

THE OLD LADY: You are not as insensitive as you might wish to appear! (*Meanwhile, The Old Lady traces some* lines in pencil on a piece of paper left from the wrapping)

THE THIEF: What are you up to there?

THE OLD LADY: I was an art teacher. I also painted...! However, other artists painted better. I am saying this, although one knows that... every Romanian painter believes that no other Romanian painter could create a masterpiece, I am a unique case: I believe it to be possible!

THE THIEF (*walks to the window. Lifts the corner of the curtain*): Soon it will be daylight and... nothing: The people are still there! Oh Lord, rain will do nicely...!

THE OLD LADY (*drawing*): Do you want something?

THE THIEF: No, darling, I wish only for a meeting!... I wish all the idiots of the town under your windows, - you believe me to be as senile as you are, if you ask me if... 'I wish for something'?!... Do you mean that I depend on you?!... (*He mumbles to himself*) You believe yourself to be great...

(*A short pause*)

THE OLD LADY: I forgot to tell you: recently. I had to deal with... Does this bother you?

THE THIEF: What?

THE OLD LADY: To tell you that I had to deal with another... thief.

THE THIEF: Here?

THE OLD LADY: No! In the park.

THE THIEF: He hit you.

THE OLD LADY: He was interested in my bag: I let him have it.

THE THIEF: Pickpocket!

THE OLD LADY: That is what I thought then.

THE THIEF (*revolted*): The idiots!... They risk for nothing. Due to them, the number of police officers increases!

THE OLD LADY: There was no problem: they caught him within the hour. I drew his face... on the calendar from the desk of the police officer.

THE THIEF: I don't understand what you are saying you did there.

THE OLD LADY: When he attacked me, I was under a street lamp: I saw his features! (…) The painter had great admiration for the way in which I could draw. Here! (*She lifts the piece of paper*) I drew you smiling! I remembered a moment of joy which made you extraordinarily human!... isn't it good?

THE THIEF: Oi! Do I look like this? Ha, ha, ha! I've never looked at myself! Especially like this!... I, when I look in the mirror, I am interested in looking tough. This is different! (…) Do you see me like this?

Th OLD LADY: This is how I see you.

THE THIEF: Thank you!... Though I suspect... You wanted to do me a good deed, tell me straight!

THE OLD LADY: I drew you: that is all! Without fear. Moreover, without suspicion!

THE THIEF: As far as I understand art!

THE OLD LADY: Yes, art! When I was drawing you, I was keen on you. I wanted to save you, and I convinced myself that you were really the one I was looking at, the one I believed in...

THE THIEF: When you drew the pickpocket at the police station, were you still so fond of him?

THE OLD LADY: I drew him as beautiful as an angel because I wanted him to be good...!

THE THIEF: When you sell me, you might be torn by love!

THE OLD LADY: You are insulting me when you are insinuating like this. I prefer to hear you swear.

THE THIEF: He, he..., I only said it...! You are such an intellectual, aren't you...! When I was a child, I happened to come across a hedgehog in the snow. For the first time in my life, I felt compassion rioting within me. I wanted to stop his suffering with a fork: a rusty object, which was leaving rusty marks in my palms - it was wet, with its tail warmed up by a sunray... I impaled the fork into its back, pressing the hedgehog into the snow - hastily, crying, and with obstinacy: but it continued to struggle. Then, I tried again with a red poker from the fire: the hedgehog opened its muzzle like in the silent movies, but there wasn't any sound. I looked into its eyes, small like beads: people lie; pain cannot be read in one's eyes! This will make them feel OK when they torture someone! After the hedgehog died, I was sick... My father kept on saying it was because of the smell of burning meat.

THE OLD LADY: You are making some very bizarre associations.

THE THIEF: Small, delicate and alone in your winter...! I'll feel very sick after I kill you.

THE OLD LADY: Have I done something wrong?

THE THIEF: Very much so.

THE OLD LADY: Because I showed you the drawing.

THE THIEF: So you knew!

THE OLD LADY: I wanted.

THE THIEF: Because I am about to take the painting... You could have shut up!

THE OLD LADY: Why?

THE THIEF: To live! And to sell me...

THE OLD LADY: The person who is paying you will have the time to destroy it. (*She is pointing to the painting*)

THE THIEF: Possible.

THE OLD LADY: Then...?

(*A short pause*)

THE THIEF: Weren't you afraid of me even for a moment...

THE OLD LADY: No.

THE THIEF: The others scream, they implore, they kiss my feet... And I don't harm them, but I only take what is absolutely necessary!

THE OLD LADY: They fear death.

THE THIEF: You aren't afraid.

THE OLD LADY: If there were a God, I could be fearful. The proof that it does not exist can be clearly seen on my face. Invaded by wrinkles.

THE THIEF: It means that it will be better for you. You're fed up with life. And with people's dirt. I am convinced you're in need of a helping hand!...

THE OLD LADY: I discovered people's dirt retrospectively. When it was exercised upon me, it did not touch me, because I had always been sorry for those who were trying to harm me...

THE THIEF: You mean that you feel sorry for me.

THE OLD LADY (*tired*): Now, you are trying to find a plausible reason for going ahead with what you want to do. (...) Since you entered here, I realised you are not content with who you are: first, you presented yourself as a social avenger, who wishes to impose justice. Then, I saw that you are only a small spider caught in its own web woven with too much skill. You feel how the web is sticking to your body and mind; you feel you cannot think outside it, and in despair, you are convinced that a decisive gesture might tear it away... You have not tried anything for so long and this is now an excuse for what you wish to do...

THE THIEF (*shouts*): I need to hate you!

THE OLD LADY: You'll manage. The painter and I had a special talent to create…reasons for being hated. (…) I am exhausted and I feel you are trying to hit me by surprise…

THE THIEF: You must not suffer.

THE OLD LADY: Perhaps I will have no time… to stop you that very moment: I do not wish to do you irreparable harm. I have the sensation that I've known you for a long time… I want to prevent you from being a condemned man in case I might die tonight.

(*Shouting, joyful voices, roars of laughter, the engine of an ambulance irrupt from outside. The Thief runs towards the window. The engine is revving in the street, the vehicle is moving away*)

THE THIEF: Done. It's finished…

THE OLD LADY: Aurica has given birth… Why do I have tears in my eyes? I am crying… In my chest, I feel the same burden as when carol singers come here to sing or when I see a bride or… when I hear the sigh of believers lamenting inside a church… I do not wish to be buried crying!...

THE THIEF (*looks into the street from behind the curtain*): Fine, the coast is clear! (*Towards The Old Lady*) The persons you are longing for don't exist any longer. They take shape only when you look at them. Or when you take what you need! Then… They hit you! That's why the future is only an imperfect repetition.

THE OLD LADY: I do not understand!...

THE THIEF (*irritated*): Now, you don't wish to pretend that you understand everything! (*Higher*) You provoke me to make me muddle my words! You know very well what I meant, but you are mocking at me!

THE OLD LADY: Would you please strike here! I abhor the lack of aestheticism. Would you keep that in mind! Let it be upwards so that the wound should be hidden under the breast!...

THE THIEF (*screams*): Damn you! What do you want from me? Tell me, double-dealer who informs the police, why don't you damn leave me alone?! (*He is ready to strike*)

THE OLD LADY: If you kill me, the person who sent you here would know who did it! (*The Thief is struck*) Your interest is to take me easy... To have one witness at least who will be able to testify that no one has harmed me.

THE THIEF: Wretched bitch, what are you planning in your head?

THE OLD LADY: The only way I could help you now, after you left your prints everywhere, is for me to try to stay alive. I am very tired, Mr, and it is not a good thing, because I have never experienced such tiredness. (…) I want to be of help to you... Someone knows you are here!

THE THIEF: I'll kill him.

THE OLD LADY: Do not be naïve! You cannot kill everyone who was near him. (*Tired*) You do what you want to do... The attack begins! Do not touch me... Do you know how you could help me?

THE THIEF (*firm*): What do you need?

THE OLD LADY: A phone call. To Ermine... To give me the injection...

THE THIEF: The phone is out of order. Anything else?

THE OLD LADY: Then, phone accident and emergency. Tell them that Old Lady Alice Arin...

THE THIEF: Haven't I told you that the telephone is out of order? Anything else, I said!

THE OLD LADY: I implore you: do not raise your voice!

THE THIEF: Otherwise, how do you want me to show an interest in you?

THE OLD LADY (*now and again, she loses touch with reality - fact that drives The Thief to despair*): If you cannot do anything, you are a condemned man. Forever... This object of beauty (*She points to the painting*) will play its part. I know it... I know it with every inch of my body. (...) The only deep feeling I am experiencing now is gratefulness...

THE THIEF: I'm taking you to your bedroom...

THE OLD LADY: I feel as if I am in a warm sleeping liquid...! It is as if I do not need any air... What strange things come to my mind?

THE THIEF: I don't like the way you look and react... I hope you aren't leaving me! You aren't so crazy to leave me in their hands, without even being guilty!

THE OLD LADY: As soon as possible, I must reach the hospital, if Ermine refuses... to give me the injection.

THE THIEF: How do you want me to transport you? In my pocket?! You'll be gone before I can explain it to your neighbours!... Damn your miserable life! Can't you have your eternal sleep in your own sheets, in your own bed!... what else do you want?

THE OLD LADY (*points to the alarm*)

THE THIEF: That I'm not... Tablets! Why don't you use tablets?

THE OLD LADY: Now... only injections. How everything is moving, and I have such a pain in my chest!... I don't know if I can do anything for you... though... you are... unacceptably rude to me. (...) If the tip of my nose has turned white... if the white is spreading under the eyes, nothing can be done.

THE THIEF (*is looking at her face in terror*)

THE OLD LADY (*barely laughs*): Darwin... was pointing to the difference between the reflex of running... in a state of fear... and the immobility of fear!...

THE THIEF (*mobilized*): Don't die! Please don't die now! Wait!

(He takes the clock; he runs to the alarm box and hits it forcefully. The sound bursts out overwhelmingly. The Thief keeps hitting the alarm box rhythmically, as if ringing a bell within his own nightmare)

THE OLD LADY (*coughs*): Mr… Mr…

THE THIEF: A bit more…! A bit more, be patient: if the alarm works (*The noise of the alarm bursts out devastatingly*) those policemen of yours will arrive immediately! They'll see I didn't harm you!...

THE OLD LADY: Water! I need air and water - a bit of air, if you are kind enough!

THE THIEF: Air? Get it yourself. I'll bring you water! Be a bit patient!

(He throws the clock onto the floor. He takes a cup from the table, he runs to the bathroom. While The Thief enters the bathroom, two people in civilian clothes rush into the room, pistols in their hands: one through the window, the other one breaking the door with the kick of his foot)

THE THIEF (*calls from the bathroom*): Hold on! (*He enters*) Hang on a minute…

THE FIRST CIVILIAN: Hands up! If you make a move…!

THE THIEF: Don't be stupid. I've got a cup of water in my hand!

THE SECOND CIVILIAN: If you make another move…!

THE FIRST CIVILIAN: Place the object on the table and go against the wall!

THE THIEF: OK, I'll do it. But first of all, look at The Old Lady. I must see if she is alive! (*The two civilians look at one another*)

THE FIRST CIVILIAN: Without tricks and... move!

THE OLD LADY: Less noise, please! You are disturbing me... You have promised me a bit of air...!

THE THIEF: Officer, The Old Lady is dying, don't you hear it?

THE SECOND CIVILIAN: Compassion got over him.

THE FIRST CIVILIAN: I'll count up to three! And... one... two...

THE THIEF (*causes the pistol to fly from The First Civilian's hand with one kick of his foot; The Thief walks towards The Old Lady*): be patient. It's very crowded here... Here!

(*The Old Lady holds her hand. With a blow, The Second Civilian knocks over the cup from The Thiefs's hand. The First Civilian jumps behind him. He twists The Thief's arm and handcuffs him*)

THE FIRST CIVILIAN: And the other arm!

THE THIEF (*calmly*): Here it is! You agitate yourself too much... You'd better observe that The Old Lady is dying and it's not because of me that she's on her deathbed. I've called you; I've set the alarm, so that she won't die! (...) Why are you behaving like this with a man who meant well? Don't you understand?

THE FIRST CIVILIAN (*thumps him in the face*): Shut up!

THE THIEF: So you're waiting for the old hag to die! To punish me by the virtue of your culpability! (*The two look implicitly at each other*)

THE SECOND CIVILIAN (*bursts in a strange laughter - a kind of long cough, without moving a muscle on his face, due to emotion or a routine which reveals something that* *happened before*) Hush!... He's chosen the variant! A well-known method, fine: too simple! My, my, my! Choose something else!...

THE FIRST CIVILIAN (*authoritarian*): Please!...

THE SECOND CIVILIAN (*disciplined*): But the cups on the floor?...The painting, the broken clock... (*He points to the table*) the dagger? Am I contradicting him?

THE FIRST CIVILIAN (*bored*): Good, good!... (*To The Old Lady*) Has he hit you? Has he menaced you?

THE SECOND CIVILIAN (*enraged towards The Thief*): Move over here and don't move!

THE OLD LADY (*opens her eyes*): The alarm functioned! My God, what negligence!... It was blocked. Your specialist has not been here to check it for over half a year!

THE FIRST CIVILIAN: You're wrong Madam, it works perfectly: it had barely started to ring, when we got into the car. Has he hit you, the beast?

THE OLD LADY: Is he tied up?

THE FIRST CIVILIAN: Don't worry: we're here with you! These individuals won't ever harm you, we can reassure you...! How are you feeling?

THE OLD LADY: I am a bit tired... I fought with him for almost an hour!

THE SECOND CIVILIAN (*witty, apart*): When we arrived, we lifted him from the floor: he was dead game! Hsiii!

THE FIRST CIVILIAN (*coughs menacingly*): Chm, chm!

THE SECOND CIVILIAN: Apologies!

THE OLD LADY: I was about to give up.

THE FIRST CIVILIAN (*patient, like with a child*): But with great will and effort, you've overcome your weakness and look... you've delivered him into our hands!... Don't worry, Madam, all will be well. You must rest!

200

THE OLD LADY (*to The Thief's bewilderment, stands up abruptly. Cold*): You do not understand a thing! (*She takes hold of the wrapped painting and she checks it*) Do your duty! Take him from here! I want to go to bed. I have had enough!

THE THIEF (*stunned and with hatred*): So you weren't sick at all!!?

THE OLD LADY (*smiling at him*): No.

THE FIRST CIVILIAN: Watch how you address the lady!

THE SECOND CIVILIAN: Speak politely, beast!

THE FIRST CIVILIAN: Take him to the car.

THE SECOND CIVILIAN: Move!

THE THIEF (*desperate*): Madam!... It is for the first time in my life that I accepted to sacrifice myself because I felt overwhelmed by an emotion, which, until today, I only suspected that it might exist! Tell me sincerely: is everything you told me a lie!?

THE FIRST CIVILIAN: Pay no attention to him!

THE OLD LADY (*sharp to The Thief*): I know that you would have liked it to be different, but... everything I told you... 'is' true! On the other hand, the manner in which I told you the story was only an educator's distortion...

(*The Thief is stunned*)

THE FIRST CIVILIAN: Madam, please... forgive me! I was hasty! I understand that all that happened was complicated! I assure you that the public prosecutor will untangle everything. (*Towards The Second Civilian*) Take him!

THE SECOND CIVILIAN: Straight away! (*To The Thief*) It seems that you swallowed the bait. (*He laughs as before*) Off you go, loser!...

THE OLD LADY (*who has unwrapped the painting and is looking at it happily*): Do not hold it against me. I had no other way!... And... forgive me I tried to show you another world! Look! You must remain what you are. We would not exist without the common people! (*She is looking at the painting in ecstasy*) Now, go! Must I insist?

THE THIEF (*with hatred*): Madam, you're a... (*He bends under the policeman's blow*)... as I've already said you're, since we've met! Because of these friends, I can't be more specific!... And, besides... you're also deceitful: art has never interested you one single moment!

THE SECOND CIVILIAN (*drags him towards the door*): Keep your words to yourself, parrot! (*He laughs as before*)

THE THIEF: You're protected with so much conviction! (*He snatches himself*) Let me tell her! She's protected you with so much cunning, with so much cruelty!... You believe in nothing! The fear of death has been the bread and water of your soul for a long time, until you've managed to delude yourself with... the wisdom of life, with... the love for eternal values... to put it better, with the love for this painting, which represents you, and through which you hope to pinch something, a few decades of attention at least, following your insignificant death! You're the most selfish sinner I've ever met.

THE FIRST CIVILIAN: I've asked you to be polite.

THE OLD LADY (*hurt*): Take him out!

THE FIRST CIVILIAN: Let's take the weapon with which he menaced you: he'll get five years, at least! Extra.

THE OLD LADY (*torn*): The knife, leave it here. It is... mine.

THE THIEF (*shouts*): She's lying (*Towards The Old Lady*) I want to prove to you that I'm not stupid: you won't be left with a clean conscience; you'll not lie in a wrap like an old fox creating the image of a saint about you; you'll not have the pleasure of closing your eyes and pitying the people who are crying for losing you! Learn that, because of you, I'll get harsh and long years in gaol!... Because of you, I'll torture myself with the thought that I could have been free; I'll curse you with every drop of sweat which will drop from my body; with every thing that I'll miss and with every surplus of pain! (*Towards the two civilians*) The knife is mine! (*The Second Civilian takes him out. The Thief tries to resist. From the wings*) She's the real Thief! She stole Artur Iovian's cane, with whom she slept, and who she loved... He was old, he loved her, and she doesn't know who she really is...! That's all she's been left...! She!... When she was young...! The real Thief is Alice Arin!... She's stolen from everyone! (*Silence*)

THE OLD LADY: One moment, please: Has Aurica given birth?

THE FIRST CIVILIAN...!!

THE OLD LADY: Mondan's wife?

THE FIRST CIVILIAN: Aurica?!

THE OLD LADY: Yes.

THE FIRST CIVILIAN (*confused, from the door*): I don't know anybody by this name.

THE OLD LADY: Forgive me. I am talking nonsense... What an idea!

THE FIRST CIVILIAN: You're exhausted. It doesn't matter. Good evening (*He exits*)

THE OLD LADY: Good evening... Good morning. (*She smiles feebly*) Good evening, good morning! (*A moment of quietness. One can hear the car move away. The Old Lady talks to herself as she puts things back in their place, with the exception of the panting. During her monologue, the noises of the night slip away from time to time*) Alone... The confrontation with this man, whose name I don't't even want to know, has finished me off... It's extraordinary how much rubbish one can utter when one is cornered!... (*It is not known if this refers to THE THIEF or to herself*) (...) So much still to do... At least, when I go to bed, I shall not be troubled by insomnia. (*She laughs*) I must request a certificate, which states that all these things happened to me; otherwise, no one will believe me! Not even Mr ANTON... He cannot understand such things because he is a professionist. (*She places the cups on the table; an owl can be heard nearby. A scream dies down in the park before it can be clearly perceived*) The dawn is calming down... I cannot hear him because of the cars. (...) It is time for me to have a rest. He damaged my clock. Ermine will shout because I didn't want to move with them... (*He puts her hand on her chest.*) Oh Lord! It hurts!... Sit down. Like this... Sit down properly. Relax! Yes. It's OK... I hate Ermine... Especially on Thursday, when she comes to style my hair!... She caresses my hair, and she touches my face... If she knew that this handkerchief which I am holding to wipe my saliva, which drips at the corner of my mouth, because of an aged muscle!... (*She laughs feebly*) How nice it is not to use it when Ermine is not here...! All smiles... all honey, she wipes me with her handkerchief, and she tells me: 'it's youth day today and we must be beautiful...'. She pretends to kiss me on my forehead and then she runs into the street. Her bored husband, who is waiting for her in the car, hoots her insistently: I hide behind the curtains and I laugh... I see her on the pavement getting rid of the handkerchief in disgust. Afterwards, they have a mighty argument. They disappear in a whirl of mechanical sounds. Then, I go down and I collect the handkerchief from the dustbin. I place it next to the others, inside the blue box (...) Poor Ermine; she has aged waiting for me to die...! First, she came with expensive silk handkerchiefs. Now she makes sure to have ordinary chequered bits of cloth - I suppose these are man's handkerchiefs... I am sorry but I do not have anything left to give her: I donated all the paintings. The house too! I am leaving her only the blue box on the chest of drawers. (*She chuckles*) 'As a sign of her Thursday efforts, I leave to my beloved Ermine, the blue box with everything it contains!'. Without regrets, I give up the spectacle of her imbecile amazement, when she will discover the stack of handkerchiefs! (*She laughs: she interrupts herself abruptly*) Oh, Lord! It hurts again! I must call Mr Anton. Somebody... To give me my injection... (*She lifts the receiver, and she dials a number. She realises in horror*) The telephone! Oh, Lord, it hurts...! It hurts and if... If... How stupid! Before I pretended a... now... I need it! I do not want...! Please let me live another day...! I have something very important to say to those I met tonight!... A bit longer!... (...) I have not listened to a waltz for a long time... I hear strange things!... I grasp rustle of organic matter in the wind... what dry lips, what a sticky cold tongue!... If I could sit up... You were right!... a grateful... hymn for joy... my tendons and my flesh sing – I'll let myself at the will of this unique chanting... my fingers are freezing, my eyes are swimming in sand... An overwhelming warm and implacable sadness is spreading to my inner parts: barren fall into myself, like a house that turns in its grounds and collapses; sparkle in the night from an accidental fire started by a child... I don't like how you are behaving!... And the quiet crying... The secret... eternity... is unravelling in inner time, although... The immortal people are those insignificant people who had been loved by important people. The painter loved me! (*She stretches her hand towards the painting, which when touched, slides to the floor*) That's

I! There, it's I!! (*She supports herself by her hands*) I shall live forever! I shall look how you smile... I pity you...!

(A chair is drawn back)

SUITABLE MUSIC AT THE END